THE AMOSKEAG MANUFACTURING COMPANY

A History of Enterprise on the Merrimack River

Aurore Eaton

Foreword by Robert B. Perreault

THE History PRESS

Published by The History Press
Charleston, SC 29403
www.historypress.net

Front cover, top: A boy laborer leaving work at the Amoskeag mill yard at 6:00 p.m. on May 24, 1909, photographed by Lewis Hine. *Library of Congress, Prints & Photographs Division, NCLC*; *bottom*: The manufacturing plant of the Manchester Mills, including Mill No. 2 (with tower), looking northwest, postcard circa 1901. *Collection of Robert B. Perreault.*
Back cover: The "All-American Flag" made by the Amoskeag Manufacturing Company in 1914. *Manchester Historic Association.*

First published 2015

Manufactured in the United States

ISBN 978.1.62619.774.9

Library of Congress Control Number: 2015939217

Notice: The information in this book is true and complete to the best of our knowledge. It is offered without guarantee on the part of the author or The History Press. The author and The History Press disclaim all liability in connection with the use of this book.

This book is dedicated to the memory of the late Elizabeth B. Lessard, librarian of the Manchester Historic Association. Betty inspired me and many others with her dedication to the preservation of Manchester's history and with her joy in sharing the stories she uncovered.

CONTENTS

Foreword, by Robert B. Perreault	7
Preface	9
Acknowledgements	13
1. The Merrimack River	15
2. The Eighteenth and Early Nineteenth Centuries	17
3. The First Textile Mills at Amoskeag Falls	19
4. The Original Amoskeag Companies	21
5. Amoskeag Village	25
6. The Birth of the Amoskeag Manufacturing Company	28
7. East Side or West Side?	30
8. Powering the Mill Yard	32
9. The Corporate Realm: The Mill Yard and Workers' Housing	46
10. Creating the New City	55
11. The First Mill: The Stark Manufacturing Company	63
12. The Amoskeag's Own Textile Mills	65
13. The Manchester Print Works	69
14. The Amoskeag Machine Shop	73
15. Amoskeag Steam Locomotives	75
16. Amoskeag Steam Fire Engines	77
17. Mechanics' Row	83
18. A Visit from Abraham Lincoln	86
19. The Civil War	90

Contents

20. Amoskeag Gingham 95
21. The Flywheel Disaster of 1891 102
22. Floods 105
23. The Amoskeag and Its Workers 109
24. Child Labor 123
25. The End of Prosperity 127
26. The All-American Flag 131
27. The Strike of 1922 134
28. Bankruptcy 143
29. Amoskeag Industries: Reinventing the Mill Yard 147
30. Postscript 151

Notes 155
Bibliography 163
Index 165
About the Author 175

FOREWORD

This year (2015) marks the centennial of George Waldo Browne's *The Amoskeag Manufacturing Co. of Manchester, New Hampshire: A History*, a portrait of the textile industry in the Queen City from its birth at the dawn of the nineteenth century to the beginning of World War I. Ever since, historians have relied on Browne's work as a Bible of facts concerning the company that transformed a village of a few hundred Yankee farmers and craftsmen into what local canal builder and visionary Samuel Blodget predicted would become the "Manchester of America." By the time that Browne penned his opus, Manchester reigned as one of New England's leading industrial centers with a multi-ethnic population of more than seventy thousand souls.

Because the title page of Browne's epic states that it was "Printed and Bound in the Mills of the Amoskeag Manufacturing Company," one wonders if the author wrote with the Amoskeag's powers-that-be looking over his shoulder. Also, because Browne's history ends in 1915, it obviously excludes the Amoskeag's most turbulent era, from postwar labor troubles that plagued the company to its demise in 1936.

Throughout subsequent decades, historians, journalists and students have written numerous books, articles and dissertations that have focused on one aspect or another of the Amoskeag's history. For example, the popular book *Amoskeag: Life and Work in an American Factory-City* (1978), by Tamara K. Hareven and Randolph Langenbach, features personal reminiscences of a small sample of the Amoskeag's former operatives and middle managers some forty years after the company's downfall. Likewise, Hareven's *Family*

Time, Industrial Time (1982) analyzes in a scholarly manner the lives of the Amoskeag's workforce. Yet in all that time and even up until recently, no one had produced a general updated history of the Amoskeag. At long last, thanks to Aurore (Dionne) Eaton, historians, as well as average readers who enjoy revisiting the past, now have at their disposal such a book, *The Amoskeag Manufacturing Company: A History of Enterprise on the Merrimack River*.

I first met Aurore in 1989 through our collaboration on a number of projects involving Manchester's Franco-American community. Over the years, we have continued to work together in various ways, always connected with some aspect of Manchester history. One of my favorite activities has been the annual "Mile of Mills" walking tour that Aurore developed for the Manchester Historic Association. Surrounded by the reds, oranges and yellows of the New Hampshire fall foliage mixed with the red bricks of the mills under deep blue autumn skies, we've taken Manchester residents and visitors of all ages from the Amoskeag Falls overlook to the south end of the Amoskeag Millyard. While weaving back and forth between mill buildings and the Merrimack River's east bank, we've shared both historical facts and colorful stories about life and work during Manchester's industrial heyday. I've always looked forward to this event, as it is a pleasure to work with Aurore and to share our mutual fascination with our hometown history with both longtime residents and newcomers to the city.

From page to page and chapter to chapter, all richly illustrated with vintage images from the Manchester Historic Association's vast photographic archives as well as from my personal collection, the Library of Congress and other sources, Aurore's text, much as her walking tours, leads us, her readers, on a series of field trips back through time.

Without a doubt, readers will rely on Aurore Eaton's history of the Amoskeag Manufacturing Company in much the same manner as generations past have done with George Waldo Browne's classic volume.

ROBERT B. PERREAULT
Modern Languages and Literatures Department, Saint Anselm College
Manchester, New Hampshire
Author of *Franco-American Life & Culture in Manchester, New Hampshire: Vivre la Différence* and *Manchester, New Hampshire (Postcard History Series)*

PREFACE

The availability of abundant water power from countless rivers and brooks flowing from inland hills and mountains to the Atlantic Ocean was the key to the development of the textile industry in New England in the nineteenth and early twentieth centuries. In 1793, the Slater Mill on the Blackstone River in Pawtucket, Rhode Island, became the first successful cotton yarn–spinning operation in America where water power was used in the manufacturing process. With advancements in automated machinery and the development of modern factory systems, the nascent American textile industry grew, first slowly and then with increasing speed. Numerous mill towns sprung up, creating wealth for investors and managers and providing gainful employment for many thousands of people.

This book tells the story of the Amoskeag Manufacturing Company, a corporation that played a major role in this rich history. The story takes us from the Amoskeag's early origins as a small spinning mill at Amoskeag Falls on the Merrimack River in the early nineteenth century to its closing in the midst of the Great Depression. From its incorporation as a stock corporation in 1831 through its bankruptcy in 1936, the company exerted tremendous influence over the landscape and the people of Manchester, New Hampshire. It was the city's major employer as well as a potent political force. The Amoskeag's mill yard[1] stretched over a mile along the east bank of the Merrimack River, and its operations on the west bank included two enormous mills, a steam power plant and other significant structures. The Amoskeag functioned as a land development

Amoskeag Manufacturing Company Southern Division mills, north of Granite Street, seen from the west side of the Merrimack River, circa 1890. *Manchester Historic Association.*

and power company and was also a major manufacturer of textiles. It became famous for its ginghams, and in the early twentieth century, the Amoskeag was known as the largest cotton textile plant in America. The company operated its own Machine Shop where skilled mechanics built textile equipment and machine parts. Its engineers and mechanics also manufactured some of the country's first steam locomotive engines and the famous Amoskeag Steam Fire Engines. During the Civil War, the Amoskeag produced sewing machines for shoe and boot manufacturers and rifle muskets for the Union army.

The Amoskeag Manufacturing Company controlled thousands of acres of land that enabled it to carry out its elegant and functional city plan for Manchester, which it first began developing in 1838. The company set the wheels in motion to transform a sleepy town into a modern city that would be able to adapt to the waves of societal and economic challenges that occurred over the decades. Manchester's built landscape and its infrastructure of civic and governmental institutions still reflect the progressive concepts of city building embraced by the Amoskeag's stockholders, managers and engineers.

This is also a story about the people who worked for the Amoskeag Manufacturing Company and the other corporations in the mill yard.

Many of them came to Manchester as hopeful immigrants from Ireland, Canada, Germany, Greece, England, Scotland, Sweden, Lithuania, Russia, Poland and many other countries. The story is also one of turmoil—of strikes, economic decline and bankruptcy. And in the end, it is a story of triumph as Manchester recovered from the loss of the giant corporation that was so intimately tied to its identity. Today, the history and legacy of the Amoskeag Manufacturing Company are embraced with pride.

ACKNOWLEDGEMENTS

I wish first to express my gratitude to the Manchester Historic Association, particularly to Jeffrey R. Barraclough, acting director, for providing access to the association's archives, photography, print and art collections and for permitting the use of images from these collections. This book would not have been possible without the generous assistance and cooperation of the association. I am grateful to publisher Joe McQuaid of the *New Hampshire Union Leader* for publishing "Looking Back," my weekly history column in the newspaper, which provided me with the opportunity to research and write about several topics related to the history of the Amoskeag Manufacturing Company. Some of the material in this book derives from a series of "Looking Back" articles that were published in 2012, which I use here with permission. I thank the National Archives for permission to use the Lewis Wickes Hine photographs from the National Child Labor Committee (NCLC) Collection and photographs from the Historic American Buildings Survey (HABS) collection. I am grateful to writer and historian Robert B. Perreault for his encouragement and for his generosity in sharing his vast knowledge of Manchester's history, as well as for permitting me to use several important images from his personal collection. I would like to give special thanks to Katie Orlando and Hilary Parrish, editors at The History Press, for all they have done to bring this project to fruition. I wish to thank my husband, Scott F. Eaton, for his constant support. My fascination with the history of the Amoskeag Manufacturing Company began one Saturday morning in the early 1990s when Scott and I participated in a walking tour of the Amoskeag Millyard presented by the Manchester Historic Association. It has been a wonderful journey of discovery ever since.

Chapter 1

THE MERRIMACK RIVER

The Amoskeag Manufacturing Company existed because of the enormous power of the water flowing over Amoskeag Falls on the Merrimack River in what is now Manchester. Here the Merrimack drops approximately fifty-four feet over a distance of about one-half of a mile, creating the best water-power site on the 116-mile-long river. The Merrimack River originates as the Pemigewasset River in the White Mountains of New Hampshire, which is the outlet of Profile Lake in Franconia Notch. This river travels southward from Profile Lake through the middle of New Hampshire for about 65 miles. When it reaches Franklin, it is joined by the Winnipesaukee River, a smaller stream that flows out of Lake Winnipesaukee at Laconia. At that point, the Pemigewasset becomes the Merrimack River.

The Merrimack continues flowing southward through Concord, Manchester and Nashua, New Hampshire. At Lowell, Massachusetts, it takes a turn to the east and runs northeasterly until it reaches the Atlantic Ocean at Newburyport, Massachusetts. At Amoskeag Falls, the Merrimack widens as it flows around several islands known as the Fishing Islands. Here the river courses over rocks, creating rapids. Originally, waterfalls existed above the islands where the river poured over large boulders. Many of these boulders are now under water behind the current dam, and some were blasted away by the Amoskeag Manufacturing Company in its efforts to reshape the river to meet its needs.

The Merrimack was an important food supply and transportation resource for the native peoples going back at least ten thousand years. In more recent

A painting by F. Frank Carson reproduced on the cover of the 1912 promotional booklet for Amoskeag Manufacturing Company and Manchester Chamber of Commerce. *Manchester Historic Association.*

centuries, the fishing grounds at Amoskeag Falls attracted the Penacook Indians and other bands of the Abenaki who inhabited the region. The word *Amoskeag* is believed to mean "place of many fish" in the Algonquian language of the Abenaki. Amoskeag Falls presented a natural impediment to the upriver migration of anadromous fish, which live most of their lives in the Atlantic Ocean. In the spring, they must make their way back to the inland spawning grounds where they originated. As they struggled to swim upriver over the rocks and rapids at Amoskeag Falls, the fish were easily harvested in large numbers through the use of nets and weirs.

The word *Merrimack* is believed to mean "place of strong current" in the Algonquian language. The great energy from this swift current provided the power needed for the development of the textile cities of Manchester and Nashua, New Hampshire, and Lowell, Lawrence and Haverhill, Massachusetts.

Chapter 2

THE EIGHTEENTH AND EARLY NINETEENTH CENTURIES

The area that is now Manchester was settled beginning around 1720 by two groups of European colonials, the English and the Scots-Irish. Most of the English settlers were descendants of the earliest European inhabitants of Massachusetts, including the Puritans. The Scots-Irish (Ulster Scots) were descendants of a group of Scots who had migrated from Scotland to Northern Ireland in the early seventeenth century. The Scots-Irish began coming to America in 1710. In 1719, a group led by Presbyterian minister David McGregor settled in New Hampshire in an area they called Nutfield, which was incorporated as Londonderry in 1722. This large settlement was later divided into several smaller towns, among them Derry and Derryfield (now Manchester), which was incorporated in 1751.

The settlers made their living in a variety of ways, including farming, hunting, trapping and lumbering. Fishing was an important source of food, and like other commodities, fish were used in trade and bartering. During the fishing season each spring, the local inhabitants spent a great deal of time at Amoskeag Falls, as the native peoples had done before them. Families competed for the best fishing spots, erecting platforms on the large boulders where they could station themselves with nets and hooks attached to long poles. Fights sometimes broke out over who would claim the best spots. The river yielded a bounty of American shad, sea lamprey (commonly called eels), river herring and salmon. So plentiful were the eels that they became a staple of the local diet. According to a poem published in 1856,

From the eels they formed their food in chief,
And eels were called the "Derryfield beef"![2]

The inhabitants in this area of the New Hampshire frontier operated water-powered saw- and gristmills along the banks of the Merrimack River and its tributaries, including Coos Brook, the Piscataquog River and Black Brook. A sawmill was built above Amoskeag Falls on the east bank of the river that was co-owned by John Stark[3] and his friend Samuel Blodget.[4] After the American Revolution, Blodget spent several months in Great Britain, where he became enamored of the marvels of the Industrial Revolution. He was particularly fascinated by the canal system that was used for transporting coal several miles from the coal fields to the city of Manchester, England. This coal fueled the engines that powered that city's great textile mills.

Having learned something about canal construction in England, Blodget conceived of building a transportation canal for riverboats on the east side of the Merrimack River in Derryfield that would enable boats to bypass Amoskeag Falls. It took him fourteen years to complete his project—from 1793 to 1807. Several other smaller canals were built along the Merrimack River during this time that enabled smooth boating around other areas of rocks and rapids. Boats traveling from as far north as Concord, New Hampshire, could make their way to Boston, Massachusetts, by connecting with the twenty-seven-mile-long Middlesex Canal where it met the Merrimack River near Lowell. This transportation system was a superior method of moving goods compared to overland travel by ox and horse carts, except in the winter when the river became icy and the Middlesex Canal froze.

At the head of Amoskeag Falls, Blodget constructed a wing dam[5] that fed into a basin where water was directed into his canal. The basin also served as a millpond for a large mill that he built there, which he named the "Great Sawmill—the Industry." Blodget dreamed that a thriving textile industry could be established along the banks of the Merrimack at Amoskeag Falls. He believed that someday there would arise there a great manufacturing city to rival Manchester, England. He envisioned that the mills in this city would be operated by harnessing the power of Amoskeag Falls. He often said, "As the country increases in population we must have manufactures, and here, at my canal, will be a manufacturing town that shall be the Manchester of America."[6] At the time of his death in September 1807, just a few months after the completion of his canal, there were no signs that this dream would ever be fulfilled.

Chapter 3

THE FIRST TEXTILE MILLS AT AMOSKEAG FALLS

Textile production was incorporated into the household economies of the early settlers of New England. Wool from sheep was spun into yarn for knitting and weaving. The Scots-Irish of Londonderry, New Hampshire, introduced the growing of the fibrous flax plant and the weaving of linen. Skilled Scots-Irish artisans spun the flax into yarn and wove it into sturdy cloth. This high-quality linen was used to make a variety of household goods, including sheets, coverlets, towels, shirts, petticoats and aprons. Linen yardage was traded with neighbors for merchandise and services and also sold commercially.

As the American population grew, the demand for textiles increasingly exceeded what was available through domestic production. Finer fabrics, such as fancy prints and ginghams, were imported from Europe. There, advances in mechanization made mass production of textiles possible. As raw cotton became more available in America toward the end of the eighteenth century, the idea of European-style textile mills started to take hold. New Englanders began to establish small cotton and wool textile operations outside of the home that were run at first on manpower and then on water power. These were somewhat experimental in nature.

By the early nineteenth century, there was increasing economic impetus to develop textile manufacturing in the United States. The country was decades behind Great Britain in textile manufacturing technology and in management know-how. Great Britain, wanting to stifle potential competition, prohibited the export of textile machinery and machine plans. In 1789, Samuel Slater

(1768–1835), a young emigrant from England, arrived in the United States. While working in the textile industry in England, he had memorized the designs of automated textile machines and had paid close attention to the industry's manufacturing and management processes. He found work with the firm of Almy & Brown in Rhode Island, and in 1793, he began manufacturing cotton textiles in Pawtucket using modern machinery that he had built and employing modern management techniques. Slater's accomplishments in Pawtucket were transformative.

In 1804, a carpenter named Benjamin Prichard worked on the construction of the first mechanized cotton mill in New Hampshire, built at New Ipswich in southwestern New Hampshire near the Massachusetts border. Soon afterward, Prichard bought a privilege (partial water power rights) at a sawmill on the Merrimack River at Amoskeag Falls owned by Jonas Harvey. Harvey's mill was located on the west bank of the river, in what was then Goffstown. The power for running the mill came from the river water directed to Harvey's under-shot water wheel from his wing dam.

In 1805, Prichard built a one-story wooden factory on the bluff below Harvey's sawmill that would share the water deflected by the wing dam. Jonas Harvey wrote that Prichard "dug a canal in a ledge which passed under the ways of my saw mill…I assisted in raising the frame of his mill and was the first who got upon the plate of the frame, and I distinctly remember that it looked rather dangerous, at such height above the boiling water."[7]

Prichard's mill was small, only forty feet square. He acquired mechanized spinning machinery from Samuel Slater and began to produce cotton and wool yarn. His equipment often malfunctioned, and he found it difficult to make a profit from his venture. A local man, Ephraim Stevens, bought Harvey's sawmill and converted it into a gristmill for grinding corn. He and his brother Robert took an interest in Prichard's operation. In March 1810, they gave Prichard a bond of $2,000 and agreed to pay him a yearly salary for his work. In exchange, Prichard agreed to keep the milldam in good repair.

Chapter 4

THE ORIGINAL AMOSKEAG COMPANIES

Benjamin Prichard enlisted local investors to support his enterprise, and on January 31, 1810, a company was organized under the name of Proprietors of the Amoskeag Cotton and Wool Manufactory. The investors included Prichard, James Parker and David McQuesten (of Bedford) and Samuel P. Kidder and John Stark Jr.[8] (of Derryfield). That year, a second floor was added to the factory with the goal of increasing yarn production. Weaving was "put out" to artisan weavers in the vicinity who wove the cotton fabrics in their homes on their own manual looms.

The new owners soon needed more money to keep the mill operating. They petitioned the New Hampshire legislature for an act of incorporation that would allow them to sell stock. On June 5, 1810, their private enterprise became a public stock company called the Amoskeag Cotton and Woolen Manufacturing Company. Coincidentally, at the same legislative session, the State of New Hampshire granted a request from the citizens of Derryfield to change the town's name to Manchester in honor of the late Samuel Blodget. There were only 113 taxpayers in town at that time.

The proprietors of the new corporation paid Benjamin Prichard about $800 for his building and machinery. He continued to supervise the manufacturing operations, but the general management duties fell to a series of agents, none of whom appeared to have had any experience in the textile business. There were only about a dozen stockholders at any one time, all local men, and most of these were farmers. Prichard remained optimistic and was always looking for ways to increase productivity. In 1811, he hired

The Bell Mill built at Amoskeag Village circa 1826 for the original Amoskeag Manufacturing Company. *Manchester Historic Association.*

Olney Robinson, an expert machinist from Smithfield, Rhode Island. Robinson spent the next few months building a new water-powered spinning frame to speed the production of yarn and also a machine for winding yarn into balls.

These upgrades came just in time, as demand for domestically produced textiles soon picked up because of the War of 1812. During this conflict between the United States and Great Britain, foreign imports of textiles slowed down to a trickle. The company's sudden prosperity was only temporary, however. The import trade was reestablished after the war ended in 1815. The Amoskeag Cotton and Woolen Manufacturing Company struggled through the next seven years, but it was able to make a major investment. In 1819, the company acquired the first water-powered loom to be used in this part of the state. This move was a step toward making the home-based weaving industry a thing of the past.

By 1822, most of the company's stockholders were ready to sell out. One of the directors disagreed with this course of action. He wrote to Samuel Slater at his home in Providence, Rhode Island, asking for a mortgage loan on the mill property to enable the operation to continue. Along with the letter, the director sent Slater a fine specimen of a salmon that had been caught at Amoskeag Falls. He boasted to Slater about the superb water power available at the Falls. Slater was intrigued. In 1823, he visited Amoskeag Falls to see for himself. He was impressed by what he saw, but he ultimately decided against making the loan. Instead, he went back to Rhode Island and met with one of his employees, Olney Robinson, who had worked at the mill at Amoskeag Falls a decade before. Slater convinced Robinson to buy the mill and the water power privilege. On October 22, 1822, Robinson became the sole owner of the Amoskeag Cotton and Woolen Manufacturing Company.

Although Robinson was a proficient textile machinery mechanic, he had little knowledge of manufacturing processes or management. Instead of proceeding cautiously, he immediately expanded the company's operations. He bought the former Stevens mill property and made plans to build a second textile factory on the site. He also bought hundreds of acres of land in the vicinity of the mill as a speculative venture, including the McGregor[9] farm that stretched along the banks of the Merrimack south of the company's mills.

Robinson repaired the existing mill and started work on his new factory. He soon needed more cash, so he borrowed approximately $6,000 from two textile machinery manufacturers: Larned Pitcher (who was Samuel Slater's son-in-law) of Seekonk, Massachusetts, and Ira Gay of Dunstable (now Nashua), New Hampshire. Historian George Waldo Browne wrote in 1915, "While Mr. Robinson possessed unbounded enthusiasm, which is a valuable asset, yet the men most interested in his efforts, the mortgagors, soon realized that he was not likely to be successful."[10] Robinson couldn't repay the loan, or at least not fast enough. In January 1825, Pitcher and Gay foreclosed on him and took ownership of half his buildings and machinery. In May 1825, Robinson was pushed out of the business for good when Slater bought out his remaining interest for $3,000.

Pitcher, Gay and Slater brought in three additional investors from Massachusetts: Dr. Oliver Dean of Medway, his brother-in-law Lyman Tiffany of Salisbury and Willard Sayles of Boston. In December 1825, they reorganized the enterprise under the name Amoskeag Manufacturing Company. Dean, who had given up medicine to become a textile executive, became the on-site manager, or "agent."[11] He moved to the McGregor Farm with his wife, Caroline, in 1826.

Dean installed new machinery in the original 1805 mill (now called the Old Mill) and completed construction on the unfinished mill. This became known as the Bell Mill, according to Browne, "on account of the bell which hung in its belfry, rung to call the operatives to work in the early morning, and to warn them at nine o'clock in the evening to discard the cares of the day and seek the repose of night that they might find renewed strength for another day's toil."[12]

The two-story Bell Mill was 140 feet long and 60 feet wide. It was outfitted with specialized equipment for manufacturing ticking, a heavy-duty blue-and-white striped cotton fabric used for making mattresses and pillows. The company began producing high-quality tickings under the trademark "ACA." This product became very popular, bringing a measure of recognition and prosperity to the company. The term ACA is believed to mean "Amoskeag Company A (quality)."

Dean later built a third mill, the Island Mill, on the largest of the Fishing Islands at Amoskeag Falls. The original purpose for the building was to serve as a machine shop, but the ticking business was so profitable that the building was enlarged and converted into a ticking factory.

Chapter 5

AMOSKEAG VILLAGE

As the textile operation at Amoskeag Falls grew, additional workers were required, as well as places for them to live. The company also needed facilities for storage, machine repair and shipping. The company offered good employment for skilled and unskilled laborers, both male and female, and families were encouraged to apply. The company built up a small community to support its operations, which it called Amoskeag Village.[13] Most of the construction of the wooden buildings took place in 1826. These consisted of individual houses for families, boardinghouses for individuals, machine shops, horse stables, a store, a post office and a meeting hall that was used on Sundays as a place of worship. Amoskeag Village became "a unique factory village, one of the pioneer hamlets in the country, where the mills were the magnets to draw many of the best and brightest of the sons and daughters of northern New England."[14]

Oliver Dean's notebook for 1826 indicates that he hired workers from nearby Goffstown and from other towns in the area, including Dunbarton, Manchester, Weare, Hooksett, Chester and Bow. Also, some of the operatives came from farther away in southern and western New Hampshire. His notebook included these and similar jottings: "Sally Collins of Goffstown near Eliphalet Richard's Store wishes a chance to come to work in the factory…three Archibald Girls of Hooksett wish to come to work in the mill and will do any kind of work… Daniel Brannan wishes employment as a Male Spinner."[15]

During the next few years, the company continued to manufacture ACA tickings, as well as cotton sheetings and shirtings and some worsted (wool) textiles.

A stereograph view of Amoskeag Village, the covered bridge and the arch dam, circa 1880. *Manchester Historic Association.*

According to Browne, "The three mills and their environments presented a most picturesque appearance. The oldest was beginning to show evidence of its age, while it stood so nearly overhanging the precipitous bank of rocks that it almost threatened to fall into the river. Just across the mill yard was a small machine shop and beyond this a cluster of dwellings which had recently been built by the company for the accommodation of its officials and operatives."[16]

The main north–south highway in the area ran directly by Amoskeag Village. This stage road connected Concord, New Hampshire, to Boston,

Massachusetts. Stagecoaches stopped daily at the Amoskeag Inn, located just north of the village. A post office was established in the village in 1828.

In the warm months, raw materials, machinery and supplies for the textile business were transported north from Boston by boat, and the company's finished textiles were shipped south to Boston by the same method. As there would be no bridge across the Merrimack at Amoskeag Falls until 1842,[17] it was impractical to offload or pick up goods at Blodget's canal across the river. So the company's cargo was loaded and unloaded at the commercial boathouse at Piscataquog Village,[18] located about one and a half miles south of Amoskeag Village. Goods were transported to and from the boathouse by heavy wagons pulled by ox teams. These teams were also used to carry goods to and from Boston in the winter when ice made river boating impossible.

Chapter 6

THE BIRTH OF THE AMOSKEAG MANUFACTURING COMPANY

The owners of the Amoskeag Manufacturing Company needed to decide on its future. They had daunting challenges to face. The company's profits were marginal because it was unable to better take advantage of the water power potential at Amoskeag Falls, which far surpassed that of other sites on the Merrimack River. The nature of textile manufacturing was changing rapidly, and the company needed to find a way to keep up. Lowell, Massachusetts, farther downstream on the Merrimack, was being developed into a mill city with giant brick factories that would soon render small mills like those at Amoskeag Village obsolete.

In the spring of 1831, five of the six partners met in the counting room of the Bell Mill. These were Dr. Oliver Dean, Ira Gay, Willard Sayles, Lyman Tiffany and Larned Pitcher. The elderly Samuel Slater could not be there, but he gave his proxy to Pitcher, his son-in law. The men drafted a petition that they presented to the New Hampshire legislature, requesting permission to incorporate their textile business into a stock company, with the potential to raise $1 million in cash assets. This request was granted, and the new stock company was incorporated on July 1, 1831, with the same name as its predecessor. The new Amoskeag Manufacturing Company began to bring in wealthy investors who wanted to be involved in the exciting prospect of fully developing the water power at Amoskeag Falls.

Several of the early investors of the new Amoskeag Manufacturing Company and their families would exercise control over the corporation throughout its history and would also control several other corporations that operated within the Amoskeag's mill yard. These financiers were descendants of Bostonians who had accumulated great wealth through maritime commerce and other mercantile pursuits in the eighteenth and early nineteenth centuries. Among them were men whose last names—Amory, Cabot, Lowell, Lawrence, Jackson and Appleton—marked them as among the elite of Boston.

In 1813, this group of entrepreneurs, who are often referred to as the "Boston Associates," invented a new system of textile manufacturing at Waltham, Massachusetts. This modern approach involved maintaining control over all the steps in the manufacturing process within one large plant, as well as exercising influence over the city or town that would help sustain the industrial development. This process included buying and selling land, designing or at least greatly influencing the town plan, controlling the power systems, constructing and fitting up the mills, hiring and training workers, providing workers' housing and purchasing raw materials and other supplies. This comprehensive approach, carried out on a large scale, resulted in greatly enhanced productivity combined with reduced expenses, which had the potential of generating substantial profit on a continuing basis.

The Boston Associates were so successful in Waltham that they duplicated the new system in Lowell, Massachusetts (1822), while continually making improvements. This became known as the Waltham-Lowell system. Manchester was the group's third major project along these lines and would become its largest. The Boston Associates would also be involved in the development of textile mill projects in Nashua and Dover, New Hampshire; Chicopee, Holyoke and Lawrence, Massachusetts; and Saco, Maine.

The Amoskeag Manufacturing Company was unique among the Boston Associates' projects because of the enormous control that this one company was able to exercise over an immense tract of land and over the available water power resources over a long period of time—105 years.

Chapter 7
EAST SIDE OR WEST SIDE?

After incorporating the small textile operation as a stock corporation, the Amoskeag Manufacturing Company's officials began taking steps to expand Amoskeag Village into a large-scale industrial center with textile manufacturing as the primary focus. To prevent speculation from driving up land costs, the investors didn't announce their plans to the public but instead quietly acquired several hundred acres of land in the vicinity of Amoskeag Village "to enable the Company to fortify itself for work and for the benefit of the coming metropolis."[19]

Although the initial decision had been made that development would take place on the west side of the Merrimack, the company decided to also take a look at the east side of the river to determine its potential for development. At first this didn't seem like a viable alternative. As described by historian George Waldo Browne in 1915:

> *In those days, when Amoskeag* [Village] *flourished and the West Side, with promise of future prestige, was the scene of activity and progress, across the Merrimack were acres of sand dunes, a picture of desolation framed in with a background of pitch-pine forest, and a frontage of free-running river. It is true there were a few farms scattered over the landscape, like oases in a desert, there were life and bustle along the canal, with its moving flotillas of lumber rafts and boats of merchandise; there were, too, the hustle and uproar accompanying the fisheries of the spring months; but no indication of the fulfillment of Judge Blodget's dream.*[20]

The company's engineers surveyed the terrain in Derryfield and discovered that the east bank of the river and the landscape beyond it, in fact, were more suitable for development than the hilly topography of the west side. The company soon began buying out scattered farms across the Merrimack from Amoskeag Village. Some of the property owners, including the Kidder and Stark families, were descendants of the colonial settlers of Derryfield. Other names of sellers had also been long associated with the town, including Merrill, Stevens, Davis, Wilson, Jackson, Clark, Rowell, Gamble, Hall and Barrett. The houses and other structures on their properties were sold to the Amoskeag along with the lands. Among these was the childhood home of Major General John Stark, which overlooked Blodget's canal at Amoskeag Falls.

By the end of 1834, the Amoskeag owned nearly all the property along the Merrimack from just above Amoskeag Falls southward to near the location of the current Granite Street Bridge. In total, the Amoskeag acquired about fifteen thousand acres on the east side of the river. The company set aside seven hundred acres for the future mill yard. It planned to use the remaining acreage for the creation of a new city that would support the industrial development.

Chapter 8

POWERING THE MILL YARD

From its incorporation in 1831, the Amoskeag Manufacturing Company was set up to concentrate its efforts primarily in the direction of land and water power development. As C.E. Potter wrote in his 1856 *History of Manchester*, "The plan of this Company was to furnish other companies disposed to locate here, with sites for their mills, and boarding houses; power to propel their mills; to erect mills and run them upon their own account; and at the same time to put their lands into market in lots for houses, shops and stores, and thus build up a manufacturing town, at the same time that they greatly enhanced the value of their own property."[21] The Amoskeag would create the canal system, the mill yard and the new city that would support large-scale textile manufacturing in Manchester. Other corporations would be established to produce the textiles. As the plan progressed, there was considerable overlap among the primary investors and officers of the Amoskeag and of these other companies so that overall control over the industrial development in Manchester stayed in the hands of the Boston Associates. By 1841, the Amoskeag Manufacturing Company had begun operating its own cotton mill, and it would eventually become a major textile manufacturer in its own right.

To succeed in its ambitious goals, the Amoskeag needed to secure the water power rights to the Merrimack River at Manchester and beyond. Because it owned the three textile mills at Amoskeag Village, the company had control of the water power on the west side of the river at Amoskeag Falls. In 1835 and 1836, the company obtained controlling interests in the Amoskeag Falls

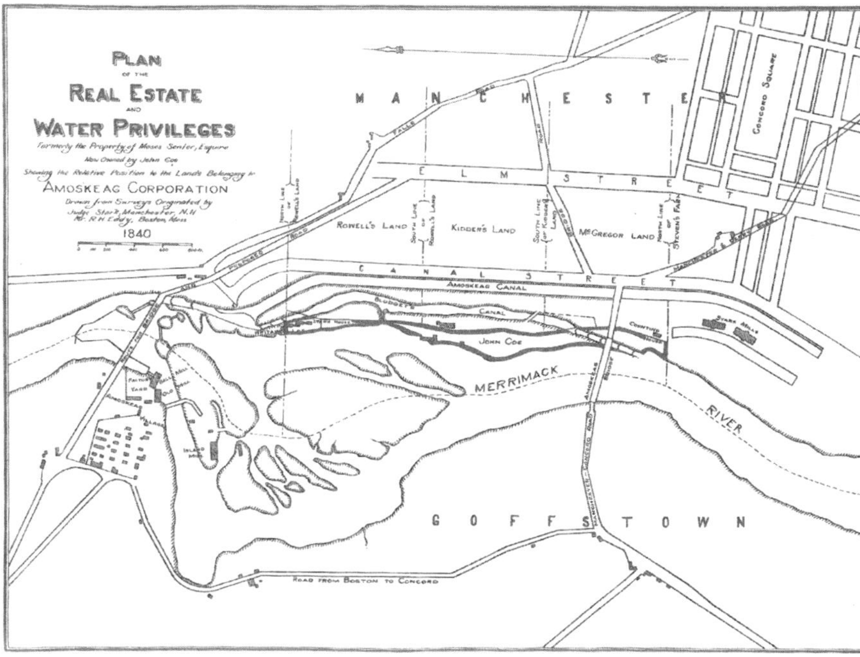

"Plan of the Real Estate and Water Privileges of the Amoskeag Corporation," 1840. *Manchester Historic Association.*

Lock and Canal Company, which operated what continued to be commonly known as Blodget's canal. This gave the Amoskeag water power rights to Amoskeag Falls on the east side of the river at the Falls. To gain control of the river north of Manchester, the company acquired interest in two textile mills, the Concord Manufacturing Company at Garvin's Falls in Bow and the Hooksett Manufacturing Company at Hooksett Falls in Hooksett. It also bought out the Isle of Hooksett Canal and the Bow Canal companies near these mills.

In addition, the company acquired the Union Locks and Canal Company that operated several transportation canals on the river downstream from Amoskeag Falls. With these moves, the Amoskeag was able to control the water power of the Merrimack River from about twenty miles north to about twenty miles south of Amoskeag Falls. In effect, "In but several months' time, the Amoskeag Company—now controlled by the Boston Associates—had grown from a small-scale producer of textiles into a veritable hydraulic empire encompassing a vast expanse of land and water in the central Merrimack valley."[22]

A view of Amoskeag Falls looking south, showing the gatehouse and the mill yard on the east side of the river (left), circa 1890. *Library of Congress, Prints & Photographs Division, HABS.*

The Amoskeag Manufacturing Company repaired the old wooden wing dams at the head of Amoskeag Falls in 1836. The dam on the west side of the river diverted water to the mills at Amoskeag Village, and the one on the east side fed water toward Blodget's canal. From 1837 to 1840, the Amoskeag erected a substantial stone dam directly above Amoskeag Falls. As part of this engineering project, the company constructed a basin to hold the river water at the head of Blodget's canal. This was situated at approximately the site of Samuel Blodget's old canal basin and millpond. This new basin included a stone retaining wall on the river side. The Amoskeag built a wooden gatehouse at the head of the basin to control the water level in the basin. This retaining wall continued northward beyond the gatehouse until it met up with the new dam. This U-shaped dam (taking its shape from the shape of the north end of Amoskeag Falls) created two channels. Similar to the effect of the original wing dam arrangement, one channel directed water into the basin on the east side of the river, and the other funneled water into a sluiceway that led to the three mills at Amoskeag Village. The dam created a giant millpond behind it that was called Amoskeag Pond. The area behind the current dam is still called this today.

Still seeking to gain more control over the flow of the Merrimack River, in 1847 the Amoskeag Manufacturing Company invested $10,000 in the Cocheco Land & Water Company, which then owned water power privileges at the outlet of Lake Winnipesaukee. This gave the company some influence over the flow of water from the lake into the Winnipesaukee River, which joined the Pemigewasset River at Franklin to become the Merrimack River. In December 1878, the Amoskeag partnered with the Boston Associates–owned manufacturing companies at Lowell and Lawrence, Massachusetts, to acquire the Winnipesaukee Lake Company. This move gave these corporations total control over the water flowing into the Winnipesaukee River from the lake, "that the water of the lake should be let down whenever needed by any company."[23] By this means, the Boston Associates could effectively control the flow of water down the entire length of the Merrimack River.

In 1849, author Henry David Thoreau (1817–1862) published *A Week on the Concord and Merrimack Rivers*, his memoir of a boating, hiking and stagecoach trip he took with his older brother John in the summer of 1839. This pleasant excursion took them from Concord, Massachusetts, to Mount Washington in the White Mountains of New Hampshire. The book includes descriptions of their boat trip on the Concord River in Massachusetts and on the Merrimack River both in Massachusetts and in New Hampshire. Thoreau wrote the book in John's memory, as he had died in 1842 at the age of twenty-seven.

Thoreau described what it was like to bypass Amoskeag Falls in the summer of 1839 through the system of locks in Blodget's canal. The canal that existed at that time was the 1816 replacement for the original 1807 canal. Though the canal was much improved over the original, its locks were difficult to negotiate, especially for the casual traveler. After passing through the canal, the brothers paddled their way into Amoskeag Pond, the "boatable part" of the Merrimack River:

> *According to the gazetteer, the descent of Amoskeag Falls, which are the most considerable in the Merrimack, is fifty-four feet in half a mile. We locked ourselves through here with much ado, surmounting the successive watery steps of this river's stair-case in the midst of a crowd of villagers, jumping into the canal to their amusement, to save our boat from upsetting, and consuming much river-water in our service. Amoskeag, or Namaskeak, is said to mean "great fishing-place." It was hereabouts that the Sachem Wannalancet resided. Tradition says that*

his tribe, when at war with the Mohawks, concealed their provisions in the cavities of the rocks in the upper part of these falls...At Amoskeag the river is divided into many separate torrents and trickling rills by the rocks, and its volume is so much reduced by the drain of the canals that it does not fill its bed.

After passing through the locks, we had poled ourselves through the canal here, about half a mile in length, to the boatable part of the river. Above Amoskeag [Falls] *the river spreads out into a lake reaching a mile or two without a bend. There were many canal boats here bound up to Hooksett, about eight miles.*[21]

In 1836, the Amoskeag began work on the first canal that would bring the water power of the Merrimack River into the planned mill yard. Originally called the Amoskeag Canal (and later known as the Upper Canal), the new watercourse was dug parallel to the river. The company would also build a second water power canal, the Lower Canal that ran between the Upper Canal and the Merrimack River. The Amoskeag couldn't make much progress on constructing the Lower Canal, however, until Blodget's transportation canal could be discontinued. The railroad was coming to Manchester, and its arrival would rapidly make river travel obsolete. When that happened, Blodget's canal would be closed and work on the Lower Canal completed.

The fate of Blodget's canal was sealed with the arrival of the first railroad train in Manchester on July 1, 1842. The tracks had been laid on the east side of the planned mill yard, running alongside the Upper Canal. Train travel was less expensive and faster than travel by riverboat, and the railroad could carry much heavier loads. Though Blodget's canal gradually fell into disuse, the Amoskeag was legally required to keep it in service. By about 1845, most of the travel remaining on the river was between Hooksett and Manchester and between Lowell, Massachusetts, and Merrimack, New Hampshire.

Thoreau wrote about the state of boat transportation in 1849, including an observation about Blodget's canal, which was then owned by the Amoskeag:

Since our voyage [in 1839] *the railroad on the bank has been extended, and there is now but little boating on the Merrimack. All kinds of produce and stores were formerly conveyed by water, but now nothing is carried up the stream, and almost wood and bricks alone are carried down, and these are also carried on the railroad. The locks are fast*

> *wearing out, and will soon be impassable, since the tolls will not pay the expense of repairing them, and so in a few years there will be an end of boating on this river.*[25]

Finally, in June 1855, the New Hampshire legislature granted permission to the Amoskeag Manufacturing Company to discontinue Blodget's canal. The company could now finish the Lower Canal and complete construction on its entire water power system. This process would take several years and would include the construction of a small gatehouse at the southwestern end of the basin (which became known as the Red Gate House) that controlled the flow of water into the Lower Canal.

The overall water power delivery system of the Amoskeag mill yard was a work of engineering genius. The Upper and Lower Canals paralleled the Merrimack River, running north to south. Water from the basin at the north end of the Amoskeag's mill yard flowed into the canals. The Upper Canal was 75 feet wide when it left the basin. Its width narrowed to 50 feet for the remainder of its 5,480-foot course. As described by Browne, "This passage

The basin looking north, showing the two gatehouses controlling water flowing into the Upper and Lower Canals, 1909. *Manchester Historic Association.*

Penstocks of new Mill Nos. 4 and 5 of the Amoskeag Manufacturing Company Central Division under construction, looking west, 1899. *Manchester Historic Association.*

Opposite, top: An aerial view of the mill yard photographed by Randolph Langenbach for the Historic American Buildings Survey, 1967. *Library of Congress, Prints & Photographs Division, HABS.*

Opposite, bottom: Looking toward the southwest from the foot of Stark Street, over the Upper Canal, circa 1870. *Library of Congress, Prints & Photographs Division, HABS.*

was walled with stones laid in the most substantial manner."[26] The Upper Canal ended near what is now the corner of Pleasant and Bedford Streets. There the water tumbled over a weir (dam) and flowed west down a short channel that emptied into the Lower Canal.

The route of Blodget's canal was roughly that of the north end of Commercial Street today, ending at about the location of the current Bridge Street Bridge. This became the route of the north end of the Lower Canal. The canal continued southward from the location of the bridge until it emptied

Looking west over the Upper Canal from Canal Street, circa 1892. *Collection of Robert B. Perreault.*

into the Merrimack River at a weir. For most of its 6,900-foot length, the Lower Canal was about 20 feet below the Upper Canal. Portions of its stone wall were extended to become part of the retaining wall on the east side of Commercial Street below the 1880 Amory Mill (now 150 Dow Street).

The way that the water power system operated was that the fast-flowing water in the canals was diverted through large pipes (penstocks) through the mill buildings lined up to their west (and sometimes through two layers of buildings). The water from the penstocks drove water wheels and turbines within the buildings. The water power energy was then transferred to textile and other types of machines through a combination of shafts, pulleys, belts and gears. The water from the buildings along the Upper Canal continued through the penstocks within the buildings and emptied into the Lower Canal. The water from the Lower Canal powered the buildings along the Merrimack River. The water that flowed through these buildings discharged into the river.

In 1871, the Amoskeag Manufacturing Company built a new dam at Amoskeag Falls, south of the original dam and closer to the gatehouse.

The gatehouse, covered bridge and arch dam, circa 1890. *Manchester Historic Association.*

View looking southeast from the west side of the Merrimack, showing the Central Division Power Plant (right) and covered footbridge, circa 1898. *Manchester Historic Association.*

Charles H. Manning, general superintendent of the Amoskeag Manufacturing Company, circa 1890. *Manchester Historic Association.*

This was called the "arch dam" because of its shape. This dam was taller than the original, enabling it to hold back more of the river's water.

The portion of the mill yard on the east side of the Merrimack would always depend on the available water power, though eventually this type of energy would be supplemented (and, in some cases, replaced) by steam and electrical power. The mill buildings and other structures that the Amoskeag built on the west side of the river used only steam power and electrical power, as water power was not available to them.

Charles H. Manning (1844–1919), who served as the general superintendent of the Amoskeag Manufacturing Company from 1882 until 1913, was instrumental in managing the company's power systems during a time when it was transitioning into the era of the steam power plants and electricity. His invention, the Manning Boiler, was used by the Amoskeag in the Northern Division Power House (built in 1909) and in power plants throughout New England. He was also the architect of the Coolidge Mill on the west side, constructed in 1909.

In 1912, the Amoskeag was operating 31 turbine water wheels with water from the Upper and Lower Canals, which generated 17,000 horsepower of energy. The company's power plants contained 203 boilers, and there were 12 steam engines, 4 steam turbines, 80 electric generators and 370 electric motors in operation. The total horsepower produced by this system was 183,100. The Amoskeag consumed over 130,000 tons of coal that year.

In 1921, the Amoskeag Manufacturing Company constructed the existing 750-foot-long concrete dam at Amoskeag Falls. The Amoskeag Dam, as it is now called, was built a short distance south of the arch dam and has a 46-foot vertical drop. The Amoskeag also rebuilt the circa

Right: Manning Boilers in the Northern Division Boiler House, invented by Charles H. Manning, circa 1910. *Manchester Historic Association.*

Below: Construction of the Amoskeag Manufacturing Company's hydroelectric power plant, 1921. *Manchester Historic Association.*

1840 wooden gatehouse on the east end of the dam as a more substantial brick structure. At the same time, the company built a hydroelectric plant on the west end of the dam to generate sixteen thousand kilowatts of electricity to power the Amoskeag's mills. The company also connected the gatehouse with the hydroelectric plant with a tunnel that runs through the dam. The construction of the new dam and power plant was a major investment made by the Amoskeag to reduce energy costs, a move that would improve its competitive stance within the textile industry. The plant was sold to Public Service Company of New Hampshire in 1936, and it is still in operation.

Opposite, top: The Amoskeag Manufacturing Company's hydroelectric plant and the Amoskeag Dam, circa 1925. *Library of Congress, Prints & Photographs Division, HABS.*

Opposite, bottom: Part of a turbine being moved from the Amoskeag Machine Shop to the new hydroelectric plant under construction, 1921. *Manchester Historic Association.*

Chapter 9

THE CORPORATE REALM

The Mill Yard and Workers' Housing

The Amoskeag Manufacturing Company acted much like a modern real estate development company does today. The Amoskeag sold land to corporations that wanted to establish textile manufacturing operations in the mill yard and leased power to them. The company also built the mills and workers' housing structures, using its own engineers as architects and its own work crews. There was a certain amount of overlapping ownership between the Amoskeag and the other textile companies operating in the mill yard, which provided a great deal of cohesion in the corporate culture that existed within the world of the Amoskeag. These other corporations included the Stark Manufacturing Company, the Amory Manufacturing Company,[27] the Manchester Mills (Merrimack Mills, Manchester Print Works) and the Langdon Mills.[28]

In 1838, the Amoskeag began construction on the east bank of the Merrimack River, building the earliest mills and workers' housing units. During the next several decades, the company was constantly building and rebuilding—shaping its corporate campus according to the needs of the times.

The construction materials used by the Amoskeag remained the same throughout its history. These included the ubiquitous red bricks that still define Manchester's profile along the Merrimack River. In the early years, these bricks came from a brickyard in Hooksett where there was a large supply of natural clay. The bricks were either floated downriver to Manchester on barges or carried by train. There was also the gray New Hampshire granite, much of which was quarried locally in east Manchester. An enormous amount of granite was used when the company straightened

View of Amoskeag workers' housing looking west down Mechanic Street toward the Stark Mill (in center, with tower), circa 1895. *Manchester Historic Association.*

A boy laborer leaving work at the Amoskeag mill yard at 6:00 p.m. on May 24, 1909, photographed by Lewis Hine. *Library of Congress, Prints & Photographs Division, NCLC.*

Mills Nos. 4 and 5 of the Amoskeag's Central Division, 1898, on the site of what is now 250 Commercial Street. *Manchester Historic Association.*

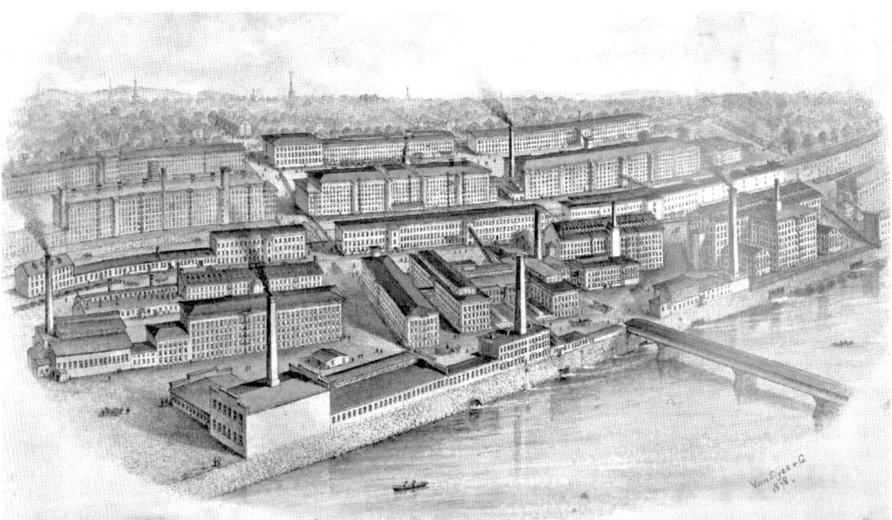

An engraving including a view of dye and bleach houses along the Merrimack River and the covered footbridge used by workers, 1878. *Manchester Historic Association.*

Opposite: The new Mill Nos. 4 and 5 under construction in 1899, now 250 Commercial Street. *Manchester Historic Association.*

out the shoreline on the east side of the river and built an impressive retaining wall. Much of the glass for windows was shipped from makers in Chelmsford, Massachusetts.

The company used large quantities of wood, including spruce, maple, birch, oak, hemlock and the sturdy southern pine that was favored for floor and ceiling beams. The Amoskeag's foundry cast the ironwork used in the mill yard and in the workers' housing buildings. The foundry-forged items included lamp posts, decorative light fixtures on the building exteriors, railings, fire hydrants, fencing and door hood brackets.

In many ways, the Amoskeag's mill yard was self-contained, as it provided services for itself that would normally come from the city. For example, the company and other corporations in the mill yard had their own fire engines and fire squads, and the company built its own reservoir to ensure there would be an adequate supply of water to fight fires.

From the 1840s on, the visual effect of the Amoskeag's mill yard and associated housing was grand by the standards of any person living in that era. By the 1860s, the sheer size of the manufacturing plant would have been overwhelming to witness, and it would only grow and become more astounding as the decades passed. By the late nineteenth century, the mill yard was a picture of efficiency, with bridges over the canals, railroad spurs providing easy transportation of goods, overhead walkways connecting the major structures and iron fencing and gates separating the world of the Amoskeag from the city around it. The Amoskeag-controlled property, with its integrity of architectural design and the genius of its organization, was also aesthetically pleasing. Author, documentary photographer and scholar Randolph Langenbach was inspired to write this description of the mill yard in 1968, prior to the destruction of about half of its buildings as part of the city's "urban renewal"[29] efforts that took place into the 1970s:

> *The Amoskeag plant grew almost continuously for seventy-five years…so it provides an excellent reflection of changes in architectural style and taste. But the real value of the millyard lies in its strikingly beautiful layout. Both the mills and the workers' housing are stylistically conservative for their times, and, except for a few examples of high Victorian fantasy in the towers and gateways, the buildings are remarkably plain. The reason for this restraint in the design of individual buildings becomes apparent when one enters the complex. No structure stands isolated or distinct. Instead the dense and continuous mass of red brick buildings flow together into a unified and organic whole. The millyard is open at each end, with canals and railroad tracks running through its entire length on two different levels above the river. However, instead of a long straight avenue, a gentle curve softens the rigor of the design, dividing the millyard into identifiable spaces. How much of this is the result of chance, and how much is a product of conscious design, is hard to say. But it is known that those who built the millyard had an uncommon sense of pride in the fabric of the plant, and a surprising respect for the value of what had come before their time.*[30]

The Amoskeag Manufacturing Company built a considerable number of workers' housing units between 1838 and 1916 as an integral part of its long-range plan for the development of the mill yard. The creation of the streets for the rows of workers' housing east of the mill yard was the first step in creating the grid system design for the new city. This "corporation housing" was commonly called "the corporations." Much of this housing was built to provide homes for the Amoskeag Manufacturing Company's own workers, and specific clusters of buildings were constructed for other textile companies that operated in the mill yard. A cluster of buildings was

A group playing croquet in the yard of an overseers' block on the south side of Stark Street, circa 1900. *Manchester Historic Association.*

Amoskeag workers' housing on the north side of Pleasant Street, near Canal Street, circa 1890. *Manchester Historic Association.*

New overseers' town houses, constructed in 1916 between Kidder and Hollis Streets facing Canal Street. *Manchester Historic Association.*

dedicated to mechanics and engineers of the Amoskeag Machine Shop, and the last project was a section of town houses built in 1916 for overseers and their families.

Most of the workers' housing was built between Elm, Canal, Hollis and Pleasant Streets, creating a distinct housing district. Those who lived there had a sense of security and a certain ease of living. The workplace was a short walk away, and there was quick access to many of the necessities of life, as well as opportunities for entertainment in the downtown. The railroad station was just down the street, where a person could board a train and travel to and from Boston in a day.

The designs of the workers' housing buildings varied according to the eras in which they were built. They were generally designed in a classic Greek Revival style with dormered roofs, but some of the structures built in the 1860s had Mansard roofs. The buildings constructed on the gentle slope that rises up from the mill yard were constructed in steps. Changes were made over time. Indoor plumbing replaced the outhouses that once existed in the yards; wooden ells were added to the backs of some of the buildings to provide storage space or to house the boardinghouse stoves; and porches were a twentieth-century addition.

The workers' housing scheme was hierarchal. The larger buildings were built to house the average operatives. They were either boardinghouses that suited individuals and provided a communal living experience or were tenement (apartment) buildings for families. For middle managers, or overseers, there were rows of town houses with fenced-in yards that provided a more upscale environment.

The Amoskeag provided houses for its agents. It built a fine brick home for this purpose a block west of Elm Street, on the corner of Franklin and Pleasant Streets, at

Amoskeag agent William Parker Straw's house and carriage house at the corner of Pleasant and Lincoln Streets, circa 1920. *Manchester Historic Association.*

the eastern edge of the workers' housing district. Agent William Parker Straw[31] lived in the house with his family for several years before moving to a new home on River Road in the north end of Manchester[32] in 1923. In an interview from the 1970s conducted for the book *Amoskeag*, Straw's daughter Mary (Straw) Flanders provides insight into the social strata of the Amoskeag's workers' housing district:

> *The house that we were in on Pleasant Street was a terrific house. I loved that house. I think of it often. I even dream about it every once in a while. It was the Amoskeag agent's house. It had an old stable, and there was a tennis court out in back. But I don't think mother wanted the house…She probably would have enjoyed moving to the North End. Most of her friends were in the North End. I never heard her say that by living near the millyard she was living in an inferior location, but she might have thought that. I'm sure that's why she wanted me, or us, to go to school up the other way. I went to the Straw School. The school was about a mile from home…The prime reason we went to the Straw School, even though we were in the Franklin school district, was because it had such good teachers. But I'm sure they also were good at the Franklin Street School, which was for children from Spruce Street and all the…you know, children from not really educated families…My parents didn't let me play in the corporation playground, which was way down near the* [railroad] *station. I guess they thought I had plenty to do up where I lived. But they never objected to the children from around there coming up to our yard. Never. My mother didn't think there was anything wrong with the other children, but she thought that the playground was meant for those who didn't have as many opportunities or the yard that I had. We had everything right there. We had the baseball grounds, and we had the skating rink in the winter time.*[33]

Employees originally were required to live in company housing, but many exceptions were granted. Generally, the occupants of the "corporations" tended to be native-born workers until the 1880s. After that time, immigrants began to move in, and some of the boardinghouses were transformed into tenement buildings that suited families. By 1910, only 15 to 20 percent of the workers in the Amoskeag's mill yard lived in corporation housing.

In the Amoskeag Manufacturing Company bankruptcy sale of 1936, a total of 106 workers' housing units were counted. These included the brick structures near the mill yard on the east side of Manchester and a row of wooden houses that were built on the west side on McGregor Street across from the Coolidge Mill. Much of this housing still exists.

Chapter 10
CREATING THE NEW CITY

Author Henry David Thoreau, in his 1849 memoir *A Week on the Concord and Merrimack Rivers*, compared Manchester of 1839 to the city in 1848:

> *At the time of our voyage Manchester was a village of about two thousand inhabitants, where we landed for a moment to get some cool water, and where an inhabitant told us that he was accustomed to go across the river into Goffstown for his water. But now, as I have been told, and indeed have witnessed, it contains fourteen thousand inhabitants. From a hill on the road between Goffstown and Hooksett, four miles distant, I have seen a thunder-shower pass over, and the sun break out and shine on a city there, where I had landed nine years before in the fields; and there was waving the flag of its museum, where "the only perfect skeleton of a Greenland or river whale in the United States" was to be seen.*[34]

In 1831, when the Amoskeag Manufacturing Company was chartered as a stock corporation, its business interests were located on the west side of the Merrimack River at Amoskeag Village. The small center of the town of Manchester on the opposite side of the river was located about three and a half miles southeast of Amoskeag Falls on what, in 1836, would become Mammoth Road.

As the Amoskeag Manufacturing Company embarked on creating a large-scale industrial landscape on seven hundred acres on the banks of the Merrimack in Manchester, it also simultaneously began transforming the

This detailed aerial perspective illustration of Manchester from 1876 shows the Merrimack River running north (left) to south (right) with the Amoskeag's mill yard on its east bank and the planned city stretching to the east beyond them. The grid system of streets shows the scope of the original landholdings of the Amoskeag Manufacturing Company and its orderly plan for the city's development. *Manchester Historic Association.*

Union Station, Boston & Maine Railroad, located south of Granite Street near the mill yard, completed 1898, photo circa 1905. *Manchester Historic Association.*

Union Station passenger receiving area, looking northwest, showing trolley and workers' housing along Granite Street, circa 1900. *Collection of Robert B. Perreault.*

town into a planned city on a grand scale. This city would grow with the mill yard and provide the housing, transportation, goods and services that the industrial interests and their employees would require.

There were, however, other motivations to creating the new city of Manchester. The wealthy Boston families behind the Amoskeag Manufacturing Company and the several corporations associated with it in Manchester were imbued with higher aspirations. These investors had seen firsthand the grimy industrial cities of Europe where a permanent underclass toiled in the mills and lived in deplorable conditions. They were determined that their projects would be well planned and well executed and would result in the establishment of prosperous, healthy and beautiful places where all citizens could benefit.

The Amoskeag determined that the city streets would be laid out on an orderly grid system that would continue the grid that had already been

Elm Street, looking south toward city hall, circa 1920. *Manchester Historic Association.*

established by the company immediately east of the planned mill yard on land set aside for workers' housing. The task of sketching out the street plan for Elm Street and the central part of the new business district was assigned to novice engineer eighteen-year-old Ezekiel A. Straw.[35] He had recently completed studies in practical mathematics at Philips Academy in Andover, Massachusetts, and had worked for a short time for the Lowell and Nashua Railroad. Straw had in mind that he would stay in Manchester for a few weeks and then return to his railroad job. However, he would remain in Manchester for the rest of his life and rise to the highest levels of management in the Amoskeag Manufacturing Company.

Straw plotted out the center of the new main street, Elm Street, as a broad boulevard, one hundred feet wide. The side streets would be fifty feet wide. He drew in the lots that would be sold to the highest bidders at the company's first land auction and included land for two public parks, Concord Square (later Concord Common, now Victory Park) and Merrimack Square (later Merrimack Common, now Veterans Memorial Park). The parks had a dual purpose—to provide green space for recreation and also to hold ponds that would provide water in case of fire. As the Amoskeag's city plan took shape during the next several years, the company would donate several additional parks to the city. It would also continue the grid system design for the streets. The company provided land for public schools and municipal buildings, either as donations or sold to the town at favorable prices. The company also donated free land for the establishment of churches and supported charitable organizations. For example, in 1878, the company donated a farmhouse to the Women's Aid and Relief Society to serve as the organization's first headquarters. Many of these transactions involved the recipient agreeing that the Amoskeag had reverter rights should the land cease to be used for the purposes for which it was given. This meant, for example, if a school building was no longer to be used as a school, the land would revert back to the Amoskeag's ownership. The Roman Catholic diocese declined to accept any donation of land from the Amoskeag, as it did not wish to have restrictions on the use of its properties.

The streets were surveyed and laid out. The company held its first land sale on October 24, 1838, at 10:00 a.m. in the rear of the new Stark Manufacturing Company mill, which was under construction. A total of 147 lots were sold for $300 to $600 each, all located between Elm, Hanover, Union and Lowell Streets. The buyers were required to put down 25 percent in cash and pledge to pay at least 25 percent per year on the three-year mortgage, with interest.

The deeds for the lots on the west side of Elm Street specified that only brick or stone structures with slate roofs could be built on them. This would help prevent the spread of fire that could threaten the workers' housing and the mill yard. The agreements also specified that only one structure could be built on one lot for at least twenty-five years. These types of deed restrictions would be attached to many of the lots sold by the Amoskeag through the years. Deed restrictions and reverter rights clauses were two of the methods that the Amoskeag used to control the development of the city.

In late 1838, the Amoskeag's directors voted to build a hotel and tavern in the new business district to accommodate the company's investors and officers, as well as other people with business in town. The company constructed a fine brick building at the northeast corner of Merrimack and Elm Streets, across from Merrimack Common. The business was called Shepherd's Tavern after its first manager, William Shepherd. It would later be known as the Manchester House.

Between 1838 and 1887, the Amoskeag held a total of ten large land sales. Additional smaller auctions took place in later years, and the company occasionally sold land through individual sales. In this way, the

The Manchester House (formerly Shepherd's Tavern) at the northeast corner of Elm and Merrimack Streets, across the street from Merrimack Common, 1866. *Manchester Historic Association.*

company gradually sold off around 14,300 acres of land on the east side of the Merrimack River. Its grid system design for the city was continued beyond the company's original acreage.

Construction proceeded rapidly after the first land sale in October 1838. The first private home in the new city was built in January 1839 on the northwest corner of Concord and Chestnut Streets by Mrs. Anna Hayes. Also that year, several commercial structures were built on Elm Street. The early buildings in the downtown were often two-story wooden structures. Frequently, the first floors were used for retail stores or other businesses, while the second floors provided housing for the store owners or to renters. Within a few months, larger buildings were being constructed, primarily on Elm Street, to accommodate many types of businesses and for offices for doctors, lawyers and other professionals who were moving into town.

The population of the new center of town swelled as hundreds of people arrived looking for work and places to live. In 1830, Manchester's population was 877. By 1840, it had grown to 3,235. The original center of town on Mammoth Road became obsolete, and Elm Street became the center of commerce. A bitter political struggle broke out as the old residents lost control of their town. However, there certainly was no going back to the way things were before. By the end of 1839, Manchester was beginning to organize itself into a modern city. Committees were formed to create the infrastructure that would provide the services necessary to support the needs of a growing municipality, including fire, police and health departments; a sewer system; a cemetery; a water supply; and schools.

In the summer of 1841, Manchester built a new town hall on Elm and Market Streets, at the location of the current city hall. This was a Greek Revival–style building topped by a cupola. The town bought the land from the Amoskeag. The company had offered to donate a piece of land elsewhere, but it would have had restrictions on its use, which did not suit the committee. The building was a well-designed and well-built showpiece. It was made of brick, ninety feet long and sixty-six feet wide and was topped by a cupola that included a large clock. On top of the cupola stood a large carved eagle, painted gold.

On August 12, 1844, a fire broke out on the third floor, which was used as an armory for two local militia companies, the Stark Guards and the Granite Fusiliers. The building burned to the ground. The Amoskeag's policy of allowing only brick buildings on the west side of Elm Street likely prevented the fire from spreading. The town built a new town hall that was bigger and more elaborate than the one it replaced. This was designed by prominent Boston architect Edward Shaw in the Gothic Revival style. It was completed in October 1845 and today continues to serve Manchester as its city hall. The building is recognized for its historical and architectural importance by being listed on the National Register of Historic Places.

In 1845, forty new buildings were completed in Manchester, and two hundred more were under construction. As written in publisher John B. Clarke's 1875 history of Manchester, "In the year 1845 the town took extraordinary strides in growth, and public improvement kept pace. It gradually assumed greater dignity and was fast ripening into a city."[36] In 1846, Manchester transitioned to a city form of government.

Amoskeag Village and Piscataquog Village were annexed by Manchester in 1853. By this time, many of the residents in these west side communities identified more closely with Manchester than with their own towns, which were Goffstown and Bedford, respectively. The Amoskeag Manufacturing Company owned several hundred acres of land on the west side near the neighborhood of McGregorville, which it began developing in the 1880s.

Census records for Manchester point to a story of continued growth:

1850	13,932
1860	20,107
1870	23,536
1880	32,630
1890	44,126
1900	56,987
1910	70,063
1920	78,384

The Amoskeag Manufacturing Company exercised a great deal of control over the shape of the planned city through its land deals and other contractual and legal agreements. It also wielded wide influence through its public benevolence. From 1838 into the early twentieth century, the Amoskeag deeded thirty-six plots of land to the city, large and small, for public parks, the building of schools, the construction of municipal buildings, the creation of the Valley Cemetery and other purposes. The company sold thirty-four lots to the city for a fraction of their value and, in many cases, for the consideration of a mere $1. Among the properties essentially donated to the city for the $1 payment were nearly all the public parks that exist today. The only two properties that the Amoskeag sold to the city at full value were Dorrs Pond in 1823, for $25,000, and Textile Field (later Gill Stadium) for $60,000 in 1927.

The Amoskeag's influence in Manchester included the political persuasion it could wield as the most powerful economic force in the city. It was Manchester's largest employer and largest property owner. Many of the people involved in local and even state politics were either employed by the Amoskeag or their livelihood was tied to the company indirectly.

Chapter II

THE FIRST MILL

The Stark Manufacturing Company

The first company to begin producing textiles on the east side of the river was the Stark Manufacturing Company, which was incorporated in 1838. The company was named in honor of Manchester's hero of the Revolutionary War, Major General John Stark. The Stark Manufacturing Company bought fourteen acres of land from the Amoskeag Manufacturing Company in the center of the new planned mill yard and secured an agreement to use water power from the Amoskeag Canal (later called the Upper Canal).

The business arrangement for the water power usage was determined through the leasing of mill powers. A mill power was "the right to draw thirty-eight cubic feet of water per second, where the head or face is twenty feet, and inversely proportional to this where the head is different."[37] In short, one mill power equals sixty-five horsepower. The Amoskeag built a five-story mill for the new company, Stark Mill No. 1, which was 150 feet long by 50 feet wide, with a three-story picker house attached on its south end. Raw cotton entered the building through this picker house, where it was put through picker machines that cleaned and fluffed up the cotton fibers for further processing.

Stark Mill No. 1 was completed in early 1839. According to historian Browne:

> *Upon the completion of Mill No. 1 it was at once fitted with machinery, and the manufacture of cotton goods was begun on the east bank of the Merrimack. Six tenement blocks or boarding houses, as they were called then,*

> *were also erected for the Stark Company by the Amoskeag Manufacturing Company, and the transformation of the scene on this side of the river was such as to amaze the inhabitants...Where is now Canal Street was then fitted with a plank walk, which became a popular promenade, when at the close of the summer days the operatives sought the open air, glad of the escape from a day's toil.*[38]

Later in 1839, a similar mill was built for the Stark company a short distance north of the original building, and in 1844, the two structures were connected when a third building was constructed between them. That year, the Stark Manufacturing Company used three million pounds of raw cotton and employed 450 women and 90 men.

The Amoskeag built six boardinghouses for the workers of the Stark Manufacturing Company just east of the new mill. The boardinghouses were constructed a short distance from the mill on Stark Street, one of the original streets laid out as part of the Amoskeag's scheme to create a new business center for Manchester.

Over the decades, this mill (now the Stark Mill at 400 Bedford Street) became part of a complex of buildings owned by the Stark Manufacturing Company. The company would become known for producing the heaviest cotton fabrics in the mill yard, including yardage for sheets, drillings (a fabric with a twill weave that has the characteristic diagonal lines made by the filling threads) and duck (a fabric with a plain weave that was sometimes used for sails). By the 1870s, the company was producing sixty thousand yards of cloth a day. The Stark also made 2,400 to 10,000 seamless bags each day on specialized looms invented and patented by a local mechanic, Cyrus Baldwin. The bags were woven in a circle. The yardage was cut, and the bottoms of the bags were sewn and the tops were finished off. The Stark seamless bags were very much in demand. They were extra sturdy and long-lasting, as they had no side seams that could split when the bags were filled with heavy grains or other goods.

Chapter 12

THE AMOSKEAG'S OWN TEXTILE MILLS

Once the basic infrastructure of the mill yard had been sufficiently developed, the Amoskeag's managers decided that it would be beneficial for the company to construct its own mills and to venture into large-scale textile manufacturing, rather than just hosting other corporations in the mill yard. Over the long run, the result would be that the Amoskeag would became one of the largest and most successful textile manufacturers in the United States.

In 1841, the company completed construction on its first two buildings in its new mill yard—identical brick buildings on the Upper Canal, south of the first Stark Mill, which were named Nos. 1 and 2 Amoskeag New Mills. These were designed by engineer Captain Phinehas Stevens, who had also been involved with the construction of the Stark properties. The 1841 buildings were called the "New Mills" because, at that time, the Amoskeag was still operating two of the three original wooden mills at Amoskeag Village on the west side of the Merrimack River—the Old Mill and the Bell Mill. The third mill, the Island Mill, had burned in 1840.[39]

The two new mills each measured 157 feet long by 48 feet wide and were five stories high, with wooden gabled roofs. In the 1850s, the roofs were removed, and an additional floor was added to each structure. The buildings were topped with flat roofs because these would be safer in the event of fire. In 1860, the 88-foot distance between the two buildings was filled in to create one large six-story mill (now 300 Bedford Street). Abraham Lincoln may have seen this structure being built when he visited the mill yard in

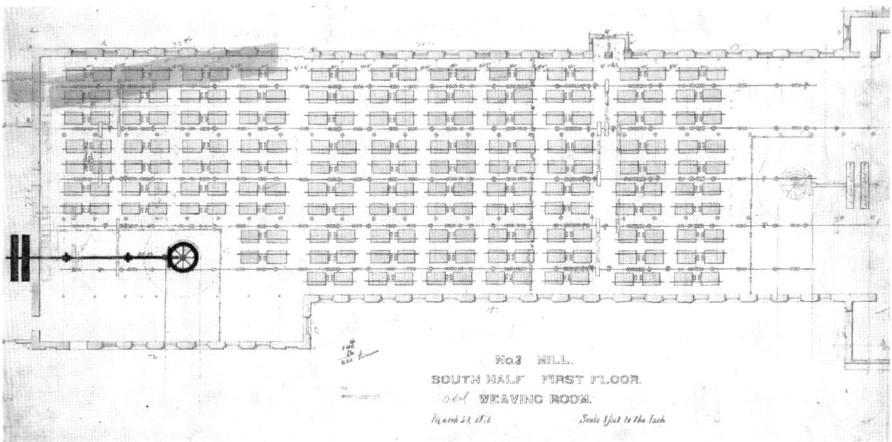

An engineering drawing of the south end of the first floor of No. 3 Amoskeag New Mill, showing the location of two turbines and two hundred looms, 1871. *Manchester Historic Association.*

March 1860. The bell tower was added later in the center of the east side of the building. It rises well above the roofline, has an open belfry and a flared hip roof covered in copper and is topped with a weather vane. The building is distinctive for having four-story picker houses at both ends that retain the original wooden loading doors on the upper floors. By the late nineteenth century, a brick annex was constructed on the west side of the building, flush with the rough granite of the Lower Canal wall.

To operate the mill, water was diverted from the Upper Canal into four penstocks that drove the four turbine water wheels that powered the machinery. In 1874, the mill employed three hundred women and one hundred men. There were five hundred looms in use for manufacturing tickings plus other heavy cotton textiles. That year, the factory produced six thousand pounds of tickings each day and three thousand pounds of finer yarns used for gingham weaving in other Amoskeag mills.

In November 1841, soon after the machinery was first started in Nos. 1 and 2 Amoskeag New Mills, a celebratory banquet took place at Shepherd's Tavern on Elm Street. The one hundred people attending raised their glasses and toasted the "Machinists and Manufacturers of Manchester." William Amory, the Amoskeag Manufacturing Company's treasurer, answered, "Distinguished for their intelligence, ability and skill, their success and the prosperity of Manchester, are cast in the same mold, forged in the same fire, and worked by the same gears, and must be run together at equal, and I hope, uninterrupted and full speed forever."[10]

In 1844, the Amoskeag Manufacturing Company constructed No. 3 Amoskeag New Mill at the end of the Upper Canal and south of Nos. 1 and 2 Amoskeag New Mills. This structure was rebuilt and enlarged in 1870. The new building was 440 feet long and five stories high. Like the earlier mills, Mill No. 3 was set up to handle the carding of raw cotton, the spinning of yarn and the weaving of the textiles. In 1874, the mill employed 350 male and 150 female workers. The mill contained eight hundred looms plus other machinery needed to transform raw cotton into the finished product. During this time, the factory primarily produced cotton denims[11] and flannels, totaling around sixty thousand pounds a week. An engine room was added to the northwest corner of the building to hold a Corliss[12] steam engine that was used as a backup when the water power from the canal was insufficient for operations. This building is now 200 Bedford Street.

During the next several decades, the Amoskeag built several other mills for its own use. Notably, these included the 1886 Jefferson Mill (now 670 North Commercial Street); the 1899 Mill No. 4 and 5, which would become known as the Waumbec Mill (250 Commercial Street); several gingham mills and related structures; and the 1864 Bag Mill, which was replaced

Workers of the "framing gang" at the construction site of the Coolidge Mill, 1909. *Manchester Historic Association.*

T. (Thomas) Jefferson Coolidge, treasurer and president of the Amoskeag Manufacturing Company, circa 1890. *Manchester Historic Association.*

by the New Bag Mill in 1915, the last mill building constructed by the Amoskeag (now 540 North Commercial Street).

Until the 1880s, the Amoskeag contained its development efforts largely to the east side of the Merrimack River, although it owned hundreds of acres of land on the west side near the McGregorville neighborhood south of Amoskeag Village. Any growth in that area needed to wait until steam power systems could be further developed (as water power was not available on the west side of the Merrimack). Also development was stalled because for thirty years there was no bridge to connect the west side with the central part of the mill yard on the east side of the river. The first bridge in Manchester had been built at that location in 1792 by local farmer Robert McGregor. The wooden structure had fallen into disrepair by 1848, and it washed away in a flood in 1851.

The Amoskeag Manufacturing Company built a new bridge there, the McGregor Bridge, in 1881.[13] The bottom of this double-decker iron bridge was used by the company and the top by the general public. The company built two large textile mills near the bridge's west end. Mill No. 11 was completed in 1889, with an addition built in 1891 (now 195 McGregor Street). Across the street to its north, the company constructed the Coolidge Mill in 1909 (now 345 McGregor Street). Both mills manufactured cotton textiles. The Amoskeag also built several wooden houses across from the Coolidge Mill for workers. The Coolidge Mill and the 1886 Jefferson Mill[14] on the east side of the river were both named in honor of T. (Thomas) Jefferson Coolidge, a longtime investor and officer of the company.[15]

The construction of these two mills was the impetus for rapid growth in this area of Manchester's west side. This was greatly encouraged by the Amoskeag's liberal land sale plan initiated in 1912 that benefited longtime employees. The Amoskeag built several other significant structures on the west side, including a power plant, storehouses, stables for its horses and a foundry.

Chapter 13

THE MANCHESTER PRINT WORKS

The Manchester Mills was one of the textile firms in the mill yard that operated as a separate corporation from the Amoskeag Manufacturing Company. It has a complicated history. The Manchester Mills was founded in 1839. Several of the company's original stockholders were also investors in the Amoskeag Manufacturing Company. The firm initially operated in Hooksett, where it manufactured mousseline de laine (also called delaine), a fine wool muslin that was used in dressmaking. The company would later also produce cotton textiles. Its specialty throughout its history was printing patterns on fabric. The Manchester Mills contracted with the Amoskeag Manufacturing Company to build a four-story mill for its operations in Manchester, which was completed in 1846.

In 1847, the Manchester Mills was reincorporated under a new charter, and its name was changed to the Merrimack Mills. The company's name was changed again in 1849 when it became the Manchester Print Works. Between 1846 and 1850, the Amoskeag constructed several additional buildings for the company (even as it was changing charters and names), as well as boardinghouses and tenement buildings nearby for its workers. Some of this housing still exists between Commercial, Granite, Bedford and Pleasant Streets.

One of the main buildings of the Manchester Prints Works was Mill No. 2, constructed in 1850. It was partially destroyed by fire in 1855 and then rebuilt. The structure was originally five and a half stories tall and had a gabled roof with dormers. Mill No. 2 had a picker house at its northwest corner that was used for the preparation of raw wool and cotton.

An engraving of No. 2 Mill of the Manchester Print Works, constructed in 1850, viewed looking north. *Manchester Historic Association.*

An example of a pattern printed on cotton cloth (calico) by the Manchester Print Works, undated. *Manchester Historic Association.*

The manufacturing plant of the Manchester Mills, including Mill No. 2 (with tower), looking northwest, postcard circa 1901. *Collection of Robert B. Perreault.*

The Manchester Print Works faced financial difficulties after the Civil War. Its manufacturing plant was sold in 1874, and the firm's name was changed back to the original Manchester Mills. The new owners invested heavily in improving the buildings and equipment and began manufacturing both wool and cotton textiles. In 1875, Mill No. 2 employed 700 women and 165 men and operated one thousand looms. The building was altered in 1879 when the gabled roof was removed in favor of a low hip roof. The plain front tower was remodeled into an elaborate Gothic Revival–style tower toward the end of the nineteenth century. This building is now 88 Commercial Street and is known as the Pandora Mill.

By 1883, the Manchester Mills employed two thousand workers. It produced a range of fabrics that included wool cassimeres, which were used for men's trousers and other clothing. The company also continued with its previous specialty of printing on fabric. It operated sixteen large roller printing machines that used engraved copper plates for printing patterns on cotton cloth. The company's textiles featured many interesting and colorful designs that reflected the fashions of the times in both dressmaking and home décor. These cotton textiles were called calicos. Advancements in the development of chemical dyes enabled the company to produce a wide range of colors and patterns. The Manchester Mills competed with other corporations in New England for the best designers, engravers and colorists.

Workers photographed in the Manchester Mills yard, circa 1875, looking south; Mill No. 2 is in the background, center. *Manchester Historic Association.*

In 1900–01, the Manchester Mills built the largest mill ever constructed in the mill yard, called the New Print Works. This gigantic U-shaped building rose directly up from the shore of the Merrimack River south of Granite Street. There was great difficulty in putting in the foundation on the sandy shore. The four-story building provided 500,000 square feet of space. The main section on the riverfront was 784 feet long. In 1903, the building employed eight hundred people and contained seventeen printing machines, each able to print twenty thousand to twenty-seven thousand pieces of cloth per week.

The construction costs for the structure exceeded estimates and caused financial problems for the company. The inability of the Manchester Mills to increase its income sufficiently to cover these costs and other expenses resulted in its sale to the Amoskeag Manufacturing Company in 1906. The Amoskeag was now able to take advantage of the printing and cloth-finishing operations housed in the building. By this time, the Amoskeag was in the process of reorganizing its management scheme in the mill yard into the Northern, Central and Southern Divisions. This building became Mill No. 10 of the Southern Division. Today, the building exists in three sections as 55 and 33 South Commercial Street and 186 Granite Street.

Chapter 14

THE AMOSKEAG MACHINE SHOP

The Amoskeag Manufacturing Company's water power, construction and textile manufacturing operations needed the services that could only be provided by a machine shop and foundry. The company created the Machine Shop Department and built its first building in 1840 on the Lower Canal. This structure was located at approximately the site of the later Machine Shop building (1890), which still exists at 400 Commercial Street.

The first shop was 260 feet long, 36 feet wide and three stories high. To the west of the building, the east bank of the Merrimack River pushed eastward to the point where the river occupied much of what is now Arms Park. At places the river at this location was 40 feet deep. In future years, the Amoskeag would carry out extensive work on both banks of the Merrimack, carting in tons of fill and straightening the river's course through the mill yard to create additional acreage for construction.

In 1842, the Amoskeag built a foundry just north of the Machine Shop to produce metal castings for a variety of purposes. Until this time, the company had purchased the castings it needed from a shop in Chelmsford, Massachusetts. According to historian George Waldo Browne, the foundry building "was considered an extravagant structure at the time, but within four years it was insufficient to meet the demands."[16] In 1848, the company built a second foundry and also erected a second Machine Shop building west of the original building.

By the mid-1860s, the Amoskeag Machine Shop operated boiler, forge and tank workshops, a pattern house and a storehouse. The department

Amoskeag foundry (right) and machine shop beyond it, looking south before construction of the retaining wall on the Merrimack River, circa 1880. *Manchester Historic Association.*

produced cotton textile machinery and turbine wheels of different sizes, from twenty to three hundred horsepower potential. The machinists also made cotton and wool carding equipment; spinning and weaving machinery; stationary steam engines; heavy tools; and heavy metal castings for a variety of uses. Each year, the operation used over 3,500 tons of iron, copper, brass and steel and consumed 1,200 tons of coal, 500 bushels of charcoal, 4,000 gallons of oil and 1,200 cords of wood. Historian C.E. Potter described the Machine Shop as being "unpretending in appearance, and entirely out of sight of all passers by…it being merely an appendage to the company's factory operations. Yet it ever has been an establishment of importance, using immense quantities of raw material, turning out a great amount of machinery, and giving employment to a large number of workmen; and now has not only become a most important part of the Amoskeag company's establishment, but has gained a worldwide reputation for the excellency of its machinery."[17]

Chapter 15

AMOSKEAG STEAM LOCOMOTIVES

Railroad transportation in the United States began to be developed in the 1820s. The railroad was both faster and less expensive than overland transportation and travel by inland canals and rivers. There was rapid growth in the creation of rail lines from the 1830s into the 1860s. A pressing demand for locomotive engines and cars developed, feeding a manufacturing boom.

By 1848, the Amoskeag Manufacturing Company Machine Shop was meeting the company's needs and also had an excess of production capacity. The Amoskeag decided to delve into steam locomotive manufacturing both to keep its mechanics busy and for the potential profit. There was money to be made, as well as prestige to be earned, in a high-profile, competitive business. Several firms in New England also began to manufacture steam locomotive engines, including machine shops in Boston, Lawrence and Taunton, Massachusetts.

The Amoskeag's first order came from the Northern Railroad in 1848. The company built a forty-six-thousand-pound engine with an iron-domed boiler, called the Etna. This powerful steam locomotive rolled out of the Machine Shop at 2:00 p.m. on March 1, 1849, and was delivered to Concord, New Hampshire, in May. The second Amoskeag engine, the General Stark, was finished in June 1849, also for the Northern Railroad. The third, the Washington, was completed in December 1849 for the Manchester & Lawrence Railroad.

The Amoskeag's engines were favorably received, so the company decided to step up production. The customer list included the major railroad

An advertising lithograph of an Amoskeag steam locomotive showing the Amoskeag mill yard in the background, circa 1850. *Manchester Historic Association.*

companies in the eastern and central United States and eastern Canada, including the Concord & Claremont; Vermont Central; New York & Erie; Ogsdenburg; Michigan Central; Michigan Southern; Passumpsic; Buffalo & State Line; Chicago & Galena; Rochester & Syracuse; Nashua & Lowell; Rutland & Burlington; St. Lawrence & Atlantic; Ohio & Pennsylvania; Northern Indiana; Adroscoggin; and Contoocook Valley.

By the end of 1857, the Amoskeag Manufacturing Company was winding down its locomotive manufacturing business. Its last customer was the Grand Trunk Railway in Maine. From September 1857 to February 1858, the Amoskeag delivered 12 engines to Portland, Maine, for the Grand Trunk. From 1849 to 1858, the company built 234 steam locomotive engines. During the height of production, in the mid-1850s, the company completed 60 engines a year, each weighing twenty to thirty tons and selling for around $8,750.

Although the Amoskeag stopped making steam locomotive engines, this type of production continued in the city. In 1854, the Manchester Locomotive Works was founded, which produced steam locomotive engines on Canal Street in Manchester for several decades.

Chapter 16

AMOSKEAG STEAM FIRE ENGINES

The Amoskeag Manufacturing Company Machine Shop ceased locomotive production in February 1858. In July of that year, Ezekiel Straw was given control of the Machine Shop. This additional responsibility made him the top manager for the entire company, as in previous years he had been put in charge of the Amoskeag's real estate, water power and manufacturing operations.[48] Straw, a civil engineer, was always looking for innovative ways to increase the company's reach and profitability, especially if it involved technological innovation. Under his leadership, the Machine Shop would next take on the exciting challenge of manufacturing steam fire engines. Straw could see that the man-powered fire engines, known as "handtubs," would eventually be replaced by the powerful steam fire engines that were just making their debut.

One man would prove to be vital to the Amoskeag's venture into steam fire engine manufacturing—Nehemiah S. Bean. Bean was born in 1818 in Gilmanton, New Hampshire. When he was a young boy, his family sent him off to live with the Shakers in Canterbury, New Hampshire, so that he could learn skills that would be useful to him in life. He left the Shakers when he was a young man. After training in the wheelwright's trade, he worked in a machine shop in Lowell, Massachusetts, and learned carpentry in Lawrence, Massachusetts. The Amoskeag Manufacturing Company hired Nehemiah in 1847 to oversee the pattern-making function at the Machine Shop. In 1850, he was put in charge of the steam locomotive department. In 1854, he left for a similar position with the Essex Manufacturing Company in Lawrence, Massachusetts.

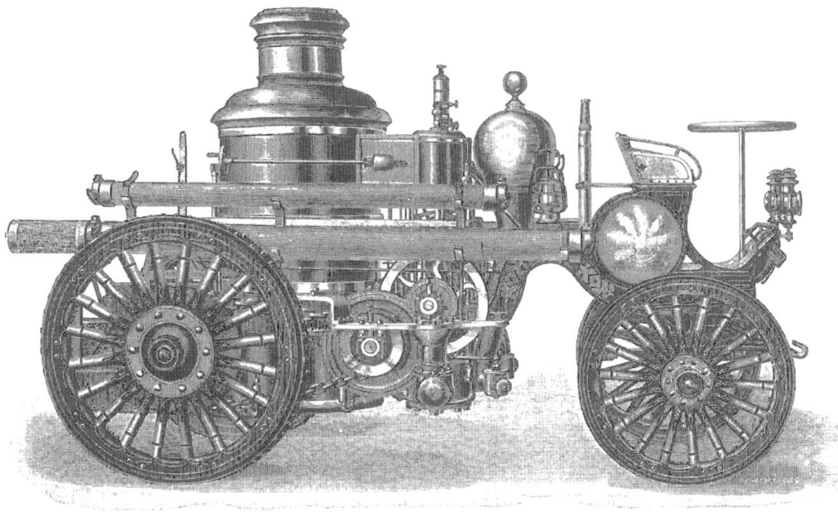

Double extra first size self-propelling Amoskeag Steam Fire Engine, engraving circa 1875. *Manchester Historic Association.*

A four-wheel Amoskeag hose carriage, to be drawn by hand, engraving circa 1875. *Manchester Historic Association.*

When work slowed down during the national Panic of 1857, Bean and another mechanic, Thomas Scott, built a steam fire engine on their own in Lawrence, completing it in early 1858. They essentially invented the machine, as there were no patterns available. The engine tested well, so that

An Amoskeag Steam Fire Engine on Vine Street across from Central Fire Station, circa 1900, with Concord Common and Amherst Street in the background. *Manchester Historic Association.*

A demonstration of a self-propelled Amoskeag Steam Fire Engine on Canal Street in 1874. *Manchester Historic Association.*

summer they brought it to Boston for a series of competitive trials. There were three other engines in competition—one from Philadelphia and two from Boston. A tall flag post on Boston Common near Beacon Street was used to measure the height of the water streams from the engines. On the second day of the competition, the Bean and Scott engine was able to shoot water to a height of around 155 feet, wetting the flag at the top of the post. At the end of the trials, the two mechanics took away second prize, $300. The City of Boston bought their engine for the enormous sum of $3,500 and named it the Lawrence No. 7.

By 1858, Nehemiah Bean was back in Manchester working at the Amoskeag Machine Shop. This time, his job was to take the engine design for the Lawrence No. 7 a few steps further. The Amoskeag wanted to be able to produce the best fire engine in New England, if not in the United States. In August 1859, the Amoskeag Machine Shop completed its first engine, assembled using Bean's improved design, the Amoskeag No. 1. This was built for the City of Manchester and was demonstrated at the city's firemen's muster held on Merrimack Common on September 14–15, 1859. The machine's public display thrilled onlookers, except for the proud members of the handtub teams, some of whom had come from great distances with their machines to compete in the muster. It was obvious to any observer that the powerful new steam engines would eventually replace the handtubs, and when that occurred, far fewer men would be needed to fight fires. The 1859 firemen's muster in Manchester was the last large muster of handtubs in American history. The event has also gone down in history for the drunken riot that occurred on the evening of September 14 involving visiting firemen.

With the great success of the first Amoskeag Steam Fire Engine, Nehemiah Bean was put in charge of engine production, and he also worked continuously designing engine improvements. He would be awarded several patents by the U.S. Patent Office. Within a short period of time, the manufacture of the Amoskeag steamers and hose carriages became the major focus of the Amoskeag Machine Shop. The company hired additional mechanics to meet demand, and the shop was soon able to complete an engine within two months of receiving an order. According to historian George Waldo Browne, "Every engine sent out was warranted to be of the best material and workmanship, and a competent engineer was sent to put the machine in complete running order."[19]

The Machine Shop built a variety of fire engines. The biggest demand was for the double pump "harp" type. On these, the hexagonal cast brass frame was bolted to the pump and steam cylinder, which made it look like the frame of a harp. The first-class harp engine weighed 6,000 pounds when loaded with fuel (wood or coal) and water and was pulled by three horses. According to Browne, this engine "was often put to severe test at firemen's musters and parades, and won many prizes, becoming a general favorite."[50] The second-class harp engine weighed 5,300 pounds when fully equipped and could be pulled either by two horses or by men. The company also made a compact 4,000-pound single-pump engine used by small towns that could be pulled either by one horse or by men.

In 1867, the company began producing "self-propellers." These "horseless carriages" used steam power for locomotion as well as for pumping water. They worked quite well in some cities, but there were difficulties to overcome. The machines could reach a speed of ten to twelve miles per hour but could only travel easily over flat surfaces. They functioned poorly on snow and ice, and they were so loud that they terrified any horses in the vicinity. These machines are recorded in the annals of motor vehicle history as being some of the first vehicles to use a modern differential gear. This allowed the four wheels to move at different speeds, which made turning sharp corners possible. This improvement was first tried in 1873 on an engine destined for Detroit, Michigan, the Lafayette 1.

How good were the Amoskeag fire engines? The record for the longest distance for a steam fire engine to throw a stream of water horizontally was reportedly set when a newly built Amoskeag steamer, Engine Six of Cambridge, Massachusetts, was tested at Fresh Pond in that city in March 1891. The astounding record was 381 feet, 4½ inches.

The famous Amoskeag Steam Fire Engines were known for their effectiveness in fighting fires and were also appreciated for their beauty. The machines were bought by small towns from Maine to Oregon, as well as by large cities including New York, Boston, New Orleans, Pittsburgh, Philadelphia, Detroit, Albany and San Francisco. The Amoskeag engines were a significant factor in saving lives and property at the Great Boston Fire of November 1872 and the San Francisco earthquake and fire of April 1906. Many were acquired by the U.S. government to be used at navy yards and arsenals. They were sold around the world, including in Canada, Russia, China, Australia, Peru and Chile. The City of London bought two, which were named Queen Victoria and Princess Alexandra.

By 1876, the Amoskeag's agent, Ezekiel Straw, had grown dissatisfied with the steam fire engine business. The Amoskeag had built 550 engines since 1859, all under the direction of Nehemiah S. Bean. These sold well, but the division was not as profitable as Straw would have liked it to be. Its main purpose seemed to be to spread the fame of the Amoskeag Manufacturing Company rather than to make money. Straw decided to sell the fire engine patents to the Manchester Locomotive Works, and at the age of fifty-eight, Nehemiah Bean took the opportunity to retire. The Locomotive Works continued to manufacture the Amoskeag steamers for several more decades. This company was bought in 1901 by the American Locomotive Company, which continued to produce the engines in Manchester until 1913. The total number of Amoskeag steamers that were produced throughout its entire history was 853. Over 70 Amoskeag Steam Fire Engines continue to exist in the United States and Canada, many of which are in museums, including the Ashland No. 1 built in 1871 for the town of Ashland, Massachusetts, which is on view in the Millyard Museum in Manchester, New Hampshire.

Chapter 17
MECHANICS' ROW

Manchester's rapid growth made it a magnet for ambitious entrepreneurs engaged in the skilled trades. In 1850, the Amoskeag Manufacturing Company built a series of wooden buildings connected by brick firewalls along the Lower Canal at the north end of the mill yard. Here the company leased space and water power to a variety of small businesses. Originally called Mechanics' Mills, this strip of buildings became known as Mechanics' Row. The earliest manufacturer to move in was Benjamin S. Stokes, a maker of metal files. His shop employed fourteen men who produced over seven hundred files a week.

Most of the businesses in Mechanics' Row were small manufacturing operations. Among these were wood and machine shops that crafted carriage wheels, spokes, sashes, doors, handles, blinds and many other items. Several shops made products that were used by the textile manufacturers in the mill yard. These included spindles, bobbins, reeds, leather belting and loom harnesses. Some of these businesses produced "machine card clothing," which were strips of leather belting embedded with wire teeth that were mounted onto the cylinders of carding machines (carders). When raw cotton or wool was run through a carder, the material's fibers were pulled apart, untangled and straightened. This produced continuous ropes of fibers called sliver that would be used in the spinning process to produce yarn for weaving.

Brush maker S.A. Felton & Company got its start in Mechanics' Row. Another occupant was the Amoskeag Axe Company, which made durable axes in a range of sizes, including broad axes for lumbering. There were

The north end of the mill yard looking north showing Mechanics' Row (upper left along the canal) and the Amoskeag lumber yard, circa 1880. *Manchester Historic Association.*

two hosiery companies owned by German immigrants John Brugger and Abraham P. Olzendam that produced stockings on automated knitting machines. Brugger employed as many as 150 people in his Mechanics' Row shop and made as many as eighty thousand pairs of hose a year.

The Amoskeag wanted to be assured that it had an adequate supply of water for firefighting and other purposes and didn't want to be dependent on the city. From 1851 to 1853, the company built its own reservoir between Oak, Russell, Harrison and Blodget Streets. The Amoskeag Reservoir was 484 feet long, 232 feet wide and 17 feet deep and could hold eleven million gallons of water. Pumps located in the basement of one of the buildings in Mechanics' Row pumped water from the Merrimack River to the reservoir. The use of the reservoir was discontinued by 1950, and homes were built on the property.

The first electricity in Manchester was generated in Mechanics' Row in 1882. That year, the New England Weston Electric Light Company rented two floors of space. Using water power leased from the Amoskeag Manufacturing Company, it began operating six 10-light arc dynamos with two emergency machines as backup. The Amoskeag became one of the first customers, and soon there were 460 electric lights operating in nearby mills. The mill workers were pleased because the electric lights produced less heat than the gas lights, keeping the rooms about 20 percent cooler.

In 1885, the Manchester Electric Light Company bought New England Weston's operations. This was the beginning of the history of Public Service Company of New Hampshire, which was officially created in 1926 when five utility companies from the region merged. This included the major electric company in the city at that time, the Manchester Traction, Light and Power Company.

Mechanics' Row was dismantled in 1886 to make way for the construction of the Jefferson Mill.

Chapter 18

A VISIT FROM ABRAHAM LINCOLN

In early 1860, Abraham Lincoln of Illinois was considering running for president of the United States, but he had not yet decided to throw his hat into the ring. His 1858 Senate race against Stephen Douglas in Illinois had been closely watched. Their series of seven spirited debates famously pitted the antislavery Lincoln against the proslavery Douglas.

On February 27, 1860, Abraham Lincoln delivered one of his most notable speeches to an audience of 1,500 people at the Cooper Union[51] in New York City. His carefully written address, arguing against the spread of slavery beyond the existing slave states, was widely published and discussed. After this engagement, Lincoln traveled by train to visit his son, sixteen-year-old Robert Todd Lincoln. Bob, as his family called him, attended Phillips Exeter Academy in Exeter, New Hampshire. Considering the great success of his New York appearance, Lincoln thought it would be worthwhile to give a few speeches along the route. New Hampshire's leading Republicans learned of this opportunity and invited him to speak in support of the party's platform and its candidates running for local office. After receiving word that Lincoln would come to Manchester, local Republicans scrambled to get the word out.

Lincoln arrived at Exeter on Thursday, March 1. He met up with Bob and Bob's hometown friend and roommate George Latham. The three made their way by train north to Concord. When the train stopped at Manchester, former mayor and local Republican leader Frederick Smyth joined the party. Lincoln gave a two-hour speech that afternoon at Phenix Hall in Concord.

Abraham Lincoln, photographed by Alexander Hesler on June 3, 1860, in Springfield, Illinois. *Manchester Historic Association.*

Lincoln and his party returned to Manchester, with Smyth as their host for their visit to the city. According to author Elwin L. Page in his 1929 book *Abraham Lincoln in New Hampshire*, "When Lincoln stepped from the train at Manchester at quarter-past four, all had been done to get him an audience that a flustered editor could hurriedly conceive. But the rain continued, and there was cause enough to fear that the hall would be too large, rather than not half large enough."[52] The small train station was located near the current intersection of Pleasant and Bedford Streets. Lincoln would have seen the rows of brick workers' housing of the Manchester Print Works directly across Bedford Street to the west and the company's mills beyond them. The party took a horse carriage to the City Hotel, located on the northeast corner of Elm and Lowell Streets.

That evening, Abraham Lincoln spoke at Smyth Hall, a large auditorium in Smyth's Block on Elm Street. This building, which was part-owned by Frederick Smyth, was located a short distance south of the City Hotel on the west side of Elm Street. The event was publicized as a "Grand Republican Rally" in local newspapers and on yellow broadsides posted around town. Despite the short notice and the bad weather, more than one thousand people showed up.

Frederick Smyth had the honor of introducing Lincoln, describing him as "the next President of the United States."[53] Lincoln spoke for ninety minutes, giving, as he did in Concord, a variation of the speech he had delivered at the Cooper Union. The audience was composed of about half Democrats and half Republicans. Lincoln's rumpled appearance was disappointing. Once he started speaking, however, the audience was completely engaged. Even those whose opinions on the slave matter differed from his took great interest in what he had to say, and the next day, the local Republican-leaning newspaper, the *Daily American*, provided a glowing review of his performance.

Frederick Smyth met up with Lincoln the next morning. Lincoln expressed that he was interested in taking a tour of the mill yard. The two men first visited the Manchester Print Works, which specialized in printing elaborate designs on fabric, often using multiple colors, a highly advanced craft for this era. Lincoln was greatly impressed by the various operations.

Lincoln next visited with Ezekiel A. Straw, the agent of the Amoskeag Manufacturing Company, who was also a prominent Republican. Straw welcomed Lincoln warmly and then sent for Edwin P. Richardson, a young machinist. Richardson arrived in his dirty work clothes and was shocked to be introduced to the eloquent speaker he had heard the evening before. When Lincoln put his hand out, Richardson shrunk back, saying, "My hands are hardly fit to take yours, Mr. Lincoln!" to which Lincoln replied, "Young man, the hand of honest toil is never too grimy for Abe Lincoln to clasp!" Richardson asked if he could wash up and change out of his grimy work clothes, but Lincoln responded, "Young man, go just as you are." Richardson then led Lincoln on a two-hour tour through the mill yard. He later wrote, "The memory of those two hours that followed will never be forgotten by me. Mr. Lincoln seemed very much surprised and pleased at the work we were doing, and I found him an enjoyable companion."[54]

Later that day, Abraham Lincoln, his son Bob and George Latham left Manchester by train. Lincoln went on to give speeches in Dover and Exeter, New Hampshire. At the Republican National Convention in Chicago on May 18, 1860, Lincoln became the Republican presidential candidate, and on November 6, 1860, he was elected the sixteenth president of the United States.

While touring the Manchester Print Works in March 1860, Lincoln had been approached by John Brugger, who produced hosiery for the company. After introducing himself, Brugger presented Lincoln with a dozen pairs of stockings made in his mill. According to Frederick Smyth:

> *Accepting them with thanks, he put them under his arm, remarking that he didn't want any paper wrapped around them, but preferred carrying them as they were. The agent said to Mr. Lincoln that he gave him the stockings*

> *for the purpose of influencing him in favor of an increase of the duty on imported goods of this character when he should become President, that our home industry might be protected. Mr. Lincoln replied that he would certainly do so, and off they trudged to the railroad station.*[55]

Smyth visited Lincoln in the White House several months later. When he asked Lincoln what had become of the stockings, Lincoln replied, "I have worn out one pair, and have a second pair on now." Lincoln pulled up his pant legs to show the stockings and added, "I guess they are rather dirty!"[56]

Chapter 19

THE CIVIL WAR

On December 26, 1860, Joseph Kidder, who owned a general store in Manchester, wrote in his diary:

> *The country is daily becoming more and more unsettled. We are now in imminent peril and clouds and darkness surround us on every side. To me at present there is no sun in the heavens. I am not an alarmist by any means, but I am unable to see how the difficulties between the North and South can be settled without blood. And if this once flows, God only knows what the end shall be.*[57]

What Kidder feared most did soon occur. The Civil War would begin with the attack on Fort Sumter, which took place from April 12 to 14, 1861, when the secessionist state of South Carolina demanded that the U.S. Army abandon its fort in Charleston Harbor. In his wartime diary entries, Kidder expressed his constant despair over the fate of the Union. He supported the war effort but lamented "the awful calamity of shedding fraternal blood,"[58] as well as the suffering of the people due to economic disruption and high taxation.

At the beginning of the conflict in 1861, there was a sense of excitement in the air in Manchester as men prepared to go to war—a war that many thought would surely be short and glorious. Historian Browne told this story from the Amoskeag Machine Shop:

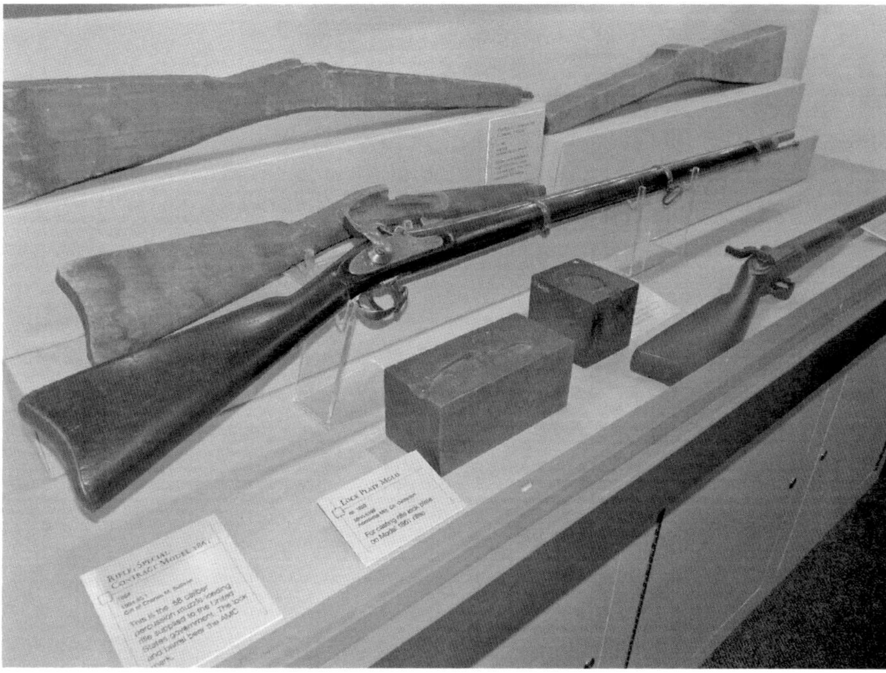

A Civil War Amoskeag rifle musket (center) in the Millyard Museum, with rough stocks, casting molds and a shotgun made from spare parts. *Manchester Historic Association.*

> *On the Fourth of July, 1861, the boys in the shops decided that it would be proper for them to show the evidence of their patriotism by displaying a flag. Accordingly they "chipped in" and bought the banner. A tree of suitable size was obtained and smoothed so as to make the staff. Then this was raised and fastened to the south wall of the old shop. There was a great deal of honest pride in this effort, and it was deemed fitting that the top should be ornamented with the design of a cannon, which was made in the shop from a pine log. The raising of the flag was a patriotic occasion, when an elaborate program was carried out. The famous Dignam's band played, and noted speakers delivered eloquent addresses suitable to the day and deed.*[59]

In September, the band's leader, Walter Dignam, joined the Fourth New Hampshire Volunteer Regiment of the Union army. As Lieutenant Dignam, he served as the leader of the regimental band. Of the twenty-four men in this band, twenty-one were from Manchester. Among them was a mechanic employed by the Amoskeag Machine Shop, Francis Harvey "Saxie" Pike.

In civilian life, he was Dignam's drum major. Saxie was already well known and admired locally and would become famous for his great showmanship as a drum major both during and after the war. He wasn't present at the Machine Shop gathering on July 4, 1861, as he was serving then in the First New Hampshire Volunteer Regiment on a short enlistment (from early May to early August 1861).

In the textile towns and cities in New England, the economic disruption that Kidder had predicted was profoundly felt. The cotton mills were completely dependent on the slave labor in the cotton fields of the South for the raw material of their industry. Over the course of the war, many had to shut down.

When the war began, the cotton textile mills in Manchester had a surplus of raw material. In September 1861, the Amoskeag Manufacturing Company, the Stark Manufacturing Company and the Manchester Print Works together had about $1 million worth of raw cotton in stock. The companies reported that they intended to continue running the mills for the benefit of the local operatives, even if they had to do so at a loss.

In April and May 1861, the Manchester Print Works made forty-eight thousand American flags in several sizes on order from the U.S. government and also produced dress patterns that used flags as part of their design. As wool remained plentiful during the war, the Print Works continued to operate at full capacity, using over three million pounds of wool a year. In 1864, it was producing twenty miles of cloth a day. The company also manufactured knitted hosiery.

Although the Amoskeag slowed down its textile operations, it continued to produce and sell a variety of cotton textiles, including denims, flannels, prints, sheetings, drills, striped shirtings and its famous ACA ticking. The denims and tickings were shipped as far away as Honolulu, Hawaii. The Stark company stayed in business by importing special machinery from Great Britain that enabled it to weave seamless bags out of linen. It also produced cotton sheetings.

The Amoskeag Machine Shop continued manufacturing steam fire engines, fulfilling orders for New York City; Milwaukee, Wisconsin; Washington, D.C.; and other cities. In April 1864, the company delivered an engine called the General Grant to Allegheny, Pennsylvania. In addition, from 1863 to 1866, the Amoskeag Machine Shop manufactured over five hundred McKay sewing machines that were used in shoe and boot making.

Even with these efforts, many workers in Manchester remained unemployed. The Amoskeag's agent, Ezekiel Straw, was determined to keep as many people on the job as possible. He traveled to Washington in December 1861 to lobby for a war contract for the Amoskeag. In early January 1862, the company won a contract to produce ten thousand Special Model 1861 rifle muskets (also known as rifled muskets) for the Union army. These were standard muzzleloading .58-caliber infantry firearms that were to be identical to the ones being manufactured at the United States Armory in Springfield, Massachusetts.

The labor force for this operation consisted of men from the Amoskeag Machine Shop and some from the cotton mills who could not serve in the army due to age or other reason, plus a few expert gunsmiths who were brought in. At any one time, two to three hundred men were employed in the gun-making process. The company used its Machine Shop buildings for production and also built a special brick structure next to the Machine Shop that it called the "armory." It was three hundred feet long and thirty feet wide and was either two or three stories high. Another building, fifty feet by forty feet, was built nearby to serve as the blacksmith shop.

The contract stipulated that the parts of the Amoskeag's guns had to be interchangeable with the parts of the Springfield guns. One of these, with the bayonet, had sixty-three parts. The manufacturing process was complex, requiring the use of at least fifteen different types of machine tools. The company made some of these tools and bought others. Straw and superintendent of the Machine Shop Nehemiah Bean had originally intended to manufacture all the gun parts in Manchester. This proved impractical, so some pieces were purchased from other shops. Notably, the Amoskeag was able to produce its own gun barrels, which required special barrel-rolling machinery and high-quality iron that was difficult to obtain.

The Amoskeag's first lot of 500 muskets was approved by government inspectors in early June 1863. Additional shipments followed, and the contract was completed by the end of February 1864. The company received its second order, which was for 15,000 rifle muskets, in September 1863. This was completed in February 1865. In November 1864, Straw asked the government to inspect an additional 2,000 musket barrels made by the Amoskeag. After they passed inspection, he asked that the company be allowed to produce an additional 2,000 guns for the government, using these barrels. This was accepted, and the order was completed in April 1865. The total number of rifle muskets produced by the Amoskeag Manufacturing Company for the Union army during the Civil War was 27,001, with the extra "1" being a sample gun that was sent to the army's Ordnance

Department in Washington. These guns were manufactured over a period of twenty-two months, at an average rate of about 1,227 per month.

The Amoskeag also made carbines that were used by the Union during the war. These were short-barreled .58-caliber firearms that were breech-loading (loaded through a chamber on the rear portion of the barrel). The particular model had been patented by inventor Edward (Eduard) Lindner of New York City in 1859. These were lightweight guns used by the cavalry. The order for carbines was placed in November 1862, and it was completed in January 1863 with 501 delivered. The company made additional Lindner carbines later on during the war that were not used by the military. It also made a sample Lindner-designed cannon that was shipped to Russia.

During the time the Amoskeag was in the gun business, "every day and sometimes several times during the day many loud reports of firearms like the firing of a platoon or whole regiment at once was heard. It was the trial of guns at the shop. Several pieces were so arranged that they could all be put to the test at once, occasioning a very loud and sharp report."[60] The *Manchester Daily American* of May 22, 1863, reported that "the company is now doing a thriving business in their manufactories for the government. The preparation was expensive but the result is said to be the best gun manufactured in New England."[61]

When violent draft riots took place in New York City from July 13 to 16, 1863, "it was rumored that an attempt was planned to seize the guns being made at the Amoskeag Company's shops. Feeling that it was safest to be prepared, Agent Straw ordered a brass field piece to be mounted at the gate just west of the lower canal and in line with Stark Street. The gun was manned by a squad of the First New Hampshire Battery, and a guard was stationed around the mill yard."[62]

Chapter 20

AMOSKEAG GINGHAM

After the Civil War ended in 1865, Ezekiel Straw, as the Amoskeag's agent, focused his attention on finding a way to put the Amoskeag Manufacturing Company in the forefront of textile manufacturing in the United States and the world. The answer was gingham.

Prior to the mid-1860s, the Amoskeag had specialized primarily in producing coarser types of cotton textiles, including tickings, sheetings, flannels and denims. The company was recognized for its high-quality products, even winning first prize in its class in the Great Exhibition in London in 1851.

During this era, most of the finer fabrics used for dressmaking and for other purposes were still being imported from Europe. American manufacturers had not yet developed the know-how to produce these types of textiles. The most popular of these was gingham, which was primarily imported from England and Scotland. Gingham is a light or medium weight cotton cloth that is produced using dyed yarn. It may be woven in plain colors or in check, stripe or plaid patterns. The production of gingham required expertise in dyeing the yarns and in setting up specialized looms to produce the desired patterns.

In July 1864, the U.S. Congress passed "An Act to Encourage Immigration" to stimulate the economy in the postwar era. Under this law, American companies were allowed to import skilled labor from abroad by paying the workers' transportation costs and by promising at least twelve months of employment. This was the opportunity that the Amoskeag needed. Ezekiel

Above: Two of the original gingham mills (in foreground) and the footbridge across the Merrimack River, looking west, circa 1905. *Manchester Historic Association.*

Left: Scottish immigrant Andrew Mungall, dye master, Amoskeag Manufacturing Company, circa 1885. *Manchester Historic Association.*

Dress gingham samples, Amoskeag Manufacturing Company, circa 1918. *Manchester Historic Association.*

Left: Ezekiel Straw, agent of the Amoskeag Manufacturing Company (1856–85), circa 1860. *Manchester Historic Association.*

Below: Students of the Varney School in Manchester posing at the entrance of the school wearing dresses made of Amoskeag gingham, 1912. *Manchester Historic Association.*

Straw; the company's treasurer, William Amory; and its New York selling agent, Gardner Brewer, visited mills in England and Scotland to learn what it would take to establish gingham production in Manchester. While abroad, Brewer made arrangements with the American Emigrant Company to bring skilled gingham weavers to the city.

At the end of 1865, a total of fifty-three women and men from Lancashire, England, immigrated to Manchester to form the nucleus of the company's new gingham department. Other skilled English workers followed, and in 1868, the company recruited forty-four experienced weavers from Scotland—all women. Like the English weavers before them, they were required to pay back their passage costs to America once they started work.

In 1870, another group of Scottish women was brought to Manchester, mostly from Glasgow and vicinity. This time, the Amoskeag required each weaver to provide a letter of reference from her pastor attesting to her fine character. A letter from a minister from Glasgow, Robert Hood, read, "This is to certify that I have known Catherine Edmond for upwards of eight years. She is sober in her habits, honest, well-conducted and trustworthy. I have perfect confidence in her."[63] A good number of these newcomers were older, experienced weavers who could train the novice mill hands.

Other skilled gingham workers from England and Scotland came to Manchester individually or with their families, bearing letters of recommendation from their former employers, family members, coworkers or clergy. Many of these remained with the Amoskeag for the remainder of their working lives, and their children often joined the company. The Scottish workers tended to reside in the brick Amoskeag workers' housing east of the mill yard.

One of Manchester's early German immigrants, Augustus Canis, was instrumental in establishing gingham production at the Amoskeag. Canis immigrated to America in 1849 and came to Manchester in 1854. Like many of the Germans who settled in Manchester, he was from Saxony, an area in eastern Germany that had a long tradition of textile manufacturing. Canis was an expert in weaving technology, and soon after his arrival, he was put in charge of the weaving departments of the Amoskeag Manufacturing Company. His expertise later proved invaluable in setting up the new gingham production departments.

A key factor in the Amoskeag's gingham production was its ability to develop beautiful and long-lasting yarn colors. Ezekiel Straw was determined to recruit the best dye masters in the world, and he found them in Scotland. In 1867, James Reid of Glasgow was hired to take over the Amoskeag's dyeing department. According to historian L. Ashton Thorp, "Mr. Straw always regarded his success in persuading this very capable man to come to this country as one of the outstanding achievements of his career and a very vital factor in the ascendancy of Amoskeag in the gingham business."[64]

Under Ezekiel Straw's leadership, the Amoskeag was able to recruit another Glasgow dye master, Andrew Mungall. He arrived in 1881 with his family. His three sons, Robert, Thomas and Samuel, served as his assistants. Thomas and Samuel would later become overseers of dyeing for the Amoskeag like their father. The area of the mill yard where the dye houses once existed is now called Mungall Street.

Straw purchased special gingham looms from Scotland and had several new buildings constructed to accommodate the gingham manufacturing processes. This included three mills built from 1868 to 1875 (now 286, 324 and 340 Commercial Street). The company also built dye houses along the riverfront behind these mills. In later years, the company would build other mills dedicated to the production of gingham.

One of the Scottish gingham weavers was Mary Cunion, born in 1885. She lived in the same corporation tenement building for sixty-eight years. Mary occupied a downstairs apartment, while her relatives lived upstairs. She was interviewed for the 1978 book *Amoskeag: Life and Work in an American Factory-City*, by Tamara K. Hareven and Randolph Langenbach:

> *I spent my happiest times in the mills. Can you beat that? I came to this house from Scotland in 1900. My Aunt Susan had it, and I've lived in this same room ever since...My Aunt Susan Cunion was in the first group that came out of Scotland. The Amoskeag sent for her...My Aunt Susan could neither read nor write...*[She] *had been a weaver over in Scotland. The Amoskeag Company hired the weavers and bought the looms, and they came together in the one boat. They brought Scottish looms...When I came in 1900, we worked from six in the morning till six at night...The ups were all right, and the downs were all right. I liked weaving...I think it's the most interesting work a girl can have. In fact, you never really learn it all...In your lifetime, there's always something new, because every warp you get in is a new one, a new color. Keeps your mind busy...For weaving you have to be clever. The colors are hard on your eyes. We used to have warps in five or six colors. You had to watch your pattern. That's why I liked it, because it takes on your brain as well as your hands.*[65]

Gingham became a staple product of the Amoskeag Manufacturing Company. By the early twentieth century, two-thirds of the company's more than twenty thousand looms were used to produce gingham. The fabric, with its many variations in patterns and colors, was highly regarded throughout the United States. However, the Amoskeag's emphasis on gingham would prove to be a handicap by the 1920s, when tastes in clothing design changed to favor other types of fabrics.

Chapter 21

THE FLYWHEEL DISASTER OF 1891

At 9:20 a.m. on the morning of October 15, 1891, the flywheel of the Big Jumbo Steam Engine exploded in its engine house on the south side of Mill No. 4 on the Lower Canal. Shattered metal was scattered over a wide area, including pieces weighing one thousand pounds. Some of this metal would later be found across the river. The brick engine house collapsed. Engineer Samuel J. Bunker and operatives Ada L. Cram and Mary Kane were killed, and several other people were badly injured.

This giant Corliss[66] engine had been installed in 1883. The flywheel was made of cast iron and was thirty feet in diameter and weighed sixty-eight tons. The engine was so remarkable that several officers of the Amoskeag Manufacturing Company included it on the tour they conducted for the delegates of the Pan-American Conference in 1889. As Frank O. Spinney of the Manchester Historic Association described in a 1948 newspaper article:

> *To stand in the engine room…and watch that wheel with its immense spokes blurring as your eyes failed to keep up with its speed made you feel the magnitude and power of the whole enterprise as no other experience could. Locked up in the whirling wheel was the equivalent and strength of 2,000 horses. From it ran great leather belts transmitting power into four adjoining mills where it operated all the machinery.*[67]

On the morning of October 15, 1891, the engine was operating as usual. With steam pressure set at ninety-five pounds per square inch, the flywheel

The aftermath of the flywheel explosion of 1891, looking west across the Merrimack River. *Manchester Historic Association.*

was revolving at sixty-one revolutions per minute. At 9:19 a.m., some unpredictable problem occurred that reduced the transfer of power from the engine to two of the mills it serviced. This caused the looms in those mills to suddenly slow down, and seconds later, the looms stopped automatically, as they were designed to do when there was a lack of energy. With no place for 75 percent of its energy to go, the flywheel began to spin faster. This caused the engine to send more energy to the looms in the other two mills. These looms, now overpowered, automatically shut down. This caused the flywheel to continue to accelerate until it finally ruptured.

The flywheel explosion of 1891 was the worst accident that had ever occurred at the Amoskeag. The event was thoroughly investigated, and it was determined that the main cause was that the flywheel had internal defects that caused it to break apart. It if had been cast properly, it would have remained intact. The wheel was replaced with a wooden one that was designed by Superintendent Charles H. Manning. It was constructed of forty-four rings of ash wood in twelve sections each. To ensure that the twenty thousand feet of timber used in the wheel would hold together, over twenty-six thousand lag bolts and screws were used to attach the pieces. Manning kept his small-scale model of the new wheel in his office as a souvenir for many years.

Chapter 22

FLOODS

The Amoskeag Manufacturing Company had gone to great lengths and great expense to acquire water power rights to the Merrimack River. To some extent, it could manage the flow of the river to the company's advantage, but it could not, in reality, control it. Floods—or, as these were generally called in the eighteenth and nineteenth centuries, freshets—were common on the river, caused by heavy rains or by snow melt. In 1741, the spray from a spring flood was seen rising fifty feet above Amoskeag Falls. There were twenty or so notable floods during the nineteenth century. The April 12–16, 1895 flood was the most extreme of these incidents up to that year, when the water rushing over the arch dam was ten feet, six inches deep. The rocks at Amoskeag Falls were completely under water, and the Jefferson Mill was flooded.

The next year, 1896, saw even greater flooding from February 28 to March 2. A two-and-a-half-day period of warm rain melted the heavy snow cover, and this was followed by a snowstorm. Cakes of ice blocking the river and high winds combined for a disastrous event. The Granite Street Bridge was swept away, as were several smaller bridges. There was widespread flooding in the mill yard.

Manchester suffered its greatest flood and its worst natural disaster in 1936. A perfect combination of weather factors led to the calamity. That winter was colder than normal in New England, and the snowfall was heavy. On March 9, a warm front moved into the region and stalled, dumping five inches of rain. A second front moved in a few days later, and the White

The late winter flood of 1896 looking north, with the chimney of the inundated Jefferson Mill power plant as a point of reference. *Manchester Historic Association.*

The March 1936 flood showing the gatehouse at the Amoskeag Dam and the hydroelectric plant across the river. *Manchester Historic Association.*

Mountains in northern New Hampshire were saturated with up to ten more inches of rain. The deep snow melted quickly, rivers began to flood and the situation was made worse by ice jams and floes.

As the incredible force of water and ice made its way south, Manchester residents watched and waited. By March 14, tons of ice could be seen crashing over the Amoskeag Dam. The worst flooding took place from March 19 to 21, when the Merrimack River reached a record high of seventeen feet, one inch above the dam. Ice floes up to eighteen inches thick crashed into bridges, houses and mill buildings. The gravel bedding under railroad tracks, trolley lines and streets gave way, and travel was disrupted for miles around.

The Granite Street Bridge was covered in three feet of water. Two large oil tanks were carried away from an island just below the dam, releasing 400,000 gallons of oil. The crumpled tanks ended up lodged against the north side of the bridge. As eyewitness William Rogier, interviewed for the *Union Leader* in 1986, recalled, "I saw 'em going down the river. They looked like three-story buildings and you could hear a tremendous bang when they hit the Granite Street Bridge. The bridge stuck. We were hoping the bridge would last, which it did."[68] The oil soaked into the walls of the flooded houses downstream, and the smell of oil in the buildings lasted for years.

The biggest fear was that the Amoskeag Dam would breach and a wall of water over fifty feet high would barrel down the river. At the site of the dam, hundreds of Works Progress Administration (WPA) workers piled sandbags to save the brick gatehouse at the head of the canal system and the hydroelectric plant on the west side of the river. The workers scrambled to safety when portions of a railway bridge from upriver crashed over the dam. Whole houses from Hooksett Village were seen floating down the river. They splintered when they hit the dam, dooming the chickens that had taken refuge on their rooftops.

Communications between the two sides of the river were largely cut off. The only working telephone line ran from the Central Fire Station downtown, through the tunnel in the Amoskeag Dam to the South Main Street firehouse on the west side. It was used only for emergencies. Shortwave radio was the only other way to get information across the Merrimack. The police department tried out its new radio equipment, and local ham operators and the National Guard got some messages through. Broadcast radio stations were still operational, so people could hear the grim news updates about the widespread flooding that was affecting not only Manchester but the entire Northeast.

In the end, the Amoskeag Dam, the gatehouse and the hydroelectric plant were saved, but Manchester lost four bridges—a steel railroad trestle south of the mill yard, the Bass Island Bridge on Second Street, the McGregor Bridge and a footbridge connecting the east and west sides of the mill yard. In addition to the Granite Street Bridge, the Amoskeag Bridge and the Queen City Bridge also miraculously survived.

As the floodwaters rose dramatically between March 19 and 21, more than 2,000 terrified city residents fled their homes. Most of the evacuations took place on the west side, but the neighborhood of Goffe's Falls in the southeastern section of Manchester was also affected. After the waters subsided, 1,500 people were left homeless in Manchester, but fortunately there was no loss of life. An emergency committee was formed to deal with the aftermath, and Mayor Damase Caron ordered that all debris be moved to dumps and burned at once to prevent the spread of disease. Both private and public concerns mobilized work crews, and around 500 WPA workers helped in the cleanup. Some buildings were demolished, and city health and building department officials inspected the remaining structures to make sure they were habitable. It took months before life returned to normal in Manchester.

In the mill yard on the east side of the river, the water had risen to fourteen feet above ground level, swamping the first floors of the mills. Windows were broken, nine hundred looms were under water and up to five feet of silt was dumped on the mill floors. The Amoskeag Manufacturing Company sustained an estimated $2,500,000 in damage to buildings and equipment. The company had closed down its operations in September 1935 and had declared bankruptcy in December. The devastating impact of the March 1936 flood would be a factor in the bankruptcy proceedings later that year.

Chapter 23

THE AMOSKEAG AND ITS WORKERS

The early workforce of the Amoskeag Manufacturing Company consisted primarily of native-born Americans who came from towns within about a fifty-mile radius of Manchester. This geographical area widened as time went on and the railroad system developed. In the early years, particularly, most of these people were of English or Scottish heritage.

A letter written by a female operative at the Manchester Print Works in 1899 gives a glimpse of what life was like for her and many women in the Amoskeag's mill yard in the nineteenth century. Mary Ann Partridge had come to Manchester from Templeton, Massachusetts, to work at the Manchester Print Works. She lived in a boardinghouse with other young women:

> *As yet I like very well. It does not tire me anymore than to do anything. Everything is clean and nice. It is true it smells a little of oil, but I can get along with that if I can make $4.50 a week. The girls wear calico dresses and sacques in the mill and big aprons. Their bonnets are none of them better looking than mine. When they go out on the street they put on their silks and rig out as nice as anyone. We have beans Sunday mornings and have had them one noon. Had cod soup and baked cod and fish hash. We have pie two or three times a day and coffee in the morning and warm biscuits. Some kind of cake and tea three times a day. They live better than I should think they could...Now do you all, all of you, write soon for a letter always does me a sight of good. More Anon—with love to all, Mary Ann.*[69]

Left: A postcard of Amoskeag workers walking west on Foundry Street, south of Mill No. 11, circa 1910. *Collection of Robert B. Perreault.*

Below: Employees of the Langdon Mills, photographed circa 1910. *Manchester Historic Association.*

Marie-Anna (St. Denis) Boucher, Amoskeag Manufacturing Company weaver, circa 1910. *Collection of Robert B. Perreault.*

As time went on, the need for mill operatives outstripped the available labor in the region so immigrant labor became the lifeblood of the Amoskeag Manufacturing Company. The Amoskeag's managers became skilled at working with people from various nationalities. The overseers learned to take advantage of the strong work ethic of the newcomers and the networks of family and social connections that they brought with them. Often entire families, from school-aged children to parents, worked together within the mill yard.

Each immigrant came to Manchester for his or her own reasons, but there were some common threads. Certainly, the search for economic opportunity was a major factor for most. Some people were escaping poverty and famine in their home countries, and others were simply looking for a new start in a place where they could broaden their potential for success in life. Some were fleeing from religious or political persecution or from war. All wished to maintain their religion, culture and traditions in America. And all were seeking the freedom to fulfill their lives and to be happy—and they wanted the same for their children.

Swedish weavers posing for a formal photograph in a Manchester studio, holding shuttles and bobbins, circa 1890. *Manchester Historic Association.*

The different immigrant groups who came to Manchester in the nineteenth and early twentieth centuries tended to develop their own ethnic neighborhoods. This was not a hard and fast rule, however, and no city neighborhood was completely homogeneous. Family connections, cultural and religious affiliations and neighborhood ties were carried into the work environment and contributed to the complex relationship structures that existed within the Amoskeag's mill yard and other workplaces in Manchester.

The first immigrant group to establish a presence in the Amoskeag's mill yard was the Irish. The first Irish millworker in Manchester was a woman who came from Lowell, Massachusetts, in 1840 to work for the Stark Manufacturing Company. By 1844, there were around six hundred Irish in the city, and by 1860, there were nearly four thousand living in Manchester out of a total population of around twenty thousand. In 1848, Reverend William McDonald, an Irish immigrant, established the first Roman Catholic church in Manchester, St. Anne Parish. The original church building was a rickety wooden structure. This was replaced by a Gothic Revival brick church, completed in 1852. The Irish community was served by Mother Frances Xavier Warde and the Sisters of Mercy, an order of nuns that she founded. On July 4, 1854, a mob stirred up by anti-immigrant sentiment

A delivery of raw cotton in the Amoskeag's mill yard, circa 1890. *Manchester Historic Association.*

threatened to burn down the church. This crisis was averted, and Manchester's transformation into a city of immigrants proceeded at full speed.

The second group of immigrants to arrive was the French-Canadians. These were French-speaking people from the province of Quebec in Canada, who would become known as the Franco-Americans. A few came to Manchester as early as 1840. After the end of the Civil War in 1865, they began arriving in larger numbers. These immigrants had the advantage of being able to easily travel back to their homes in Quebec by train. There were about 1,500 Franco-Americans living in Manchester in 1869. The Franco-Americans in Manchester were successful to a large extent in replicating the types of communities they had in Canada, which centered on their Roman Catholic parishes. By the end of the nineteenth century, textile mills in New England, including the Amoskeag, were actively recruiting French-Canadian workers because of the stability of this population. In 1910, the Franco-Americans were the largest ethnic group in Manchester, making up 38 percent of the population of the city. The spire of the Gothic Revival church of Ste. Marie Parish, completed in 1899,

A drawing-in girl of the Amoskeag Manufacturing Company setting up the harness and reeds for a loom, circa 1912. *Manchester Historic Association.*

Opposite, top: Workers in the carding room in the Jefferson Mill, circa 1900. *Collection of Robert B. Perreault.*

Opposite, bottom: Workers in a burling room of the Amoskeag Manufacturing Company; they removed knots or lumps from the fabric, circa 1911. *Manchester Historic Association.*

can be seen looming above the mills on the west side of Manchester. This parish became the nucleus of the emerging Notre Dame neighborhood.

In the federal census of 1870, nearly half the people in Manchester were listed as foreign-born, and many of those born in the United States had parents

Two workers in the Amoskeag mill yard, circa 1920. *Collection of Robert B. Perreault.*

who had been immigrants. By this time, German and Swedish immigrants, many of these skilled laborers, had started to arrive in sizeable numbers. The Amoskeag had also brought in English and Scottish immigrants to work in the gingham mills beginning in the late 1860s, but these groups were small in comparison to the population in the city. In 1882, only 2 percent of Manchester's population was from Great Britain.

Polish immigrants began arriving by the end of the nineteenth century, and by 1910, there were two thousand Poles living in Manchester; this group made up 10 percent of the Amoskeag's workforce. Greek immigration began around 1900, and around this time, Lithuanians and Russians also began arriving in Manchester, though in relatively small numbers.

In December 1912, the makeup of the employee population of the Amoskeag Manufacturing Company (which at that time totaled 15,500 workers) was as follows (a person was considered to belong to an ethnic group if he or she was an immigrant or a child of immigrants):

8 percent American
8 percent Polish
9 percent combination English, German, Scottish, Swedish, Lithuanian and Russian
11 percent Greek
13 percent Irish
51 percent French

Among the Amoskeag's workers, whether they were born in the United States or had come to Manchester from afar, one thing was common—the strong identification that employees developed toward the company. This attachment occurred for many out of a sense of pride in working for a successful corporation and also because of the Amoskeag's employment policies. The availability of good-quality, low-priced housing in the corporations, for example, was one employee benefit that was extremely important to many of the workers.

The company explained its long-term approach to dealing with its employees in the company's history published in 1915:

> *From its incorporation in 1831, the Amoskeag Manufacturing Company has believed in a liberal policy towards all. This has been shown in the favorable terms upon which land has been sold, in the generous treatment accorded the city, of which it was the god-father, wherever and whenever any public improvement was designed. To an even more marked degree has this generous spirit been displayed towards employees. The operatives have understood this fact and appreciated the consideration from the beginning. Thus the mills have been the*

Amoskeag Textile Club cooking class, 1912. *Manchester Historic Association.*

The Amoskeag Textile Club baseball team, 1913. *Manchester Historic Association.*

> *Mecca for those seeking employment of that kind, so there is not a manufacturing concern having a more intelligent type of working men and women than the great crowds that pass and repass the gates every working day in the year. Altogether the city, the employees and the Company are far more fortunate in this respect than in most manufacturing places.*[70]

As long as the company was profitable, there was certainly an altruistic component to the employee welfare programs. There were also sound business reasons to be generous. Loyal employees are more productive employees who are less likely to harbor grievances. The company's benevolence programs, also called "corporate paternalism," effectively kept unions from making much progress in the mill yard for decades.

One Amoskeag program benefited employees in the early years. The first mill in Manchester began operating in 1839, followed by others. By 1842, there was a need for a bank in town. As no one was ready to incorporate such an institution, the Amoskeag decided to hold deposits made by its employees for safekeeping. This was done for the accommodation of its workers, and not for profit, as the company had no intention of remaining in the banking business. By 1856, commercial banks were operating in Manchester, so the Amoskeag stopped accepting deposits. The company's "bank" had $175,000 of employee

Girls working in the Amoskeag's children's garden, circa 1911; workers' housing on West Merrimack Street near Canal Street is visible in the background. *Manchester Historic Association.*

money in its coffers at that time. The Amoskeag paid the employees back in full as soon as they asked for their money. With the Amoskeag paying a steady 6 percent interest, few were in a hurry to collect. It would take about twelve years before all the accounts were closed.

In 1911, the Amoskeag built a new employment office on Canal Street between Stark and Market Streets. The purpose was to consolidate the personnel functions of the company under one department. Handling the hiring, transfer, leaves and dismissal of employees was an enormous task. In one month alone, September 1912, over seven hundred people were hired. The office allowed the company to control the allocation of workers throughout the mill yard in the interest of greater efficiency. The company could now also more effectively keep any undesirable persons out of the mill yard. This included former workers who had been fired for being unreliable, unproductive or for making trouble. Also, the company could now better keep out potential labor organizers.

Simultaneous to this effort to centralize personnel functions, the company embarked on a program to organize and expand its employee welfare program. According to Hareven and Langenbach in their book *Amoskeag*, "The paternalistic measures were devised to attract additional immigrants to the city, to socialize them to industrial work, to instill loyalty to the Company, to curb labor unrest and to prevent unionization."[71]

One of the new programs created under the umbrella of corporate paternalism was the Accident Department. This was set up within the employment office to provide medical treatment to employees injured on the job. There were frequent accidents in the mill yard. Many of these were minor cuts and bruises, but others (like the flywheel disaster of 1891) were serious and even fatal. Another terrible accident occurred on March 27, 1911, when a steam pipe exploded in one of the company's power plants, killing three people.

The Accident Department included a room equipped like a hospital ward that was available to handle minor injuries that occurred in the mill yard. The medical function was staffed by two nurses, with a surgeon on call. The company also employed two additional nurses who visited employees in their homes to provide assistance where needed, including giving advice to new mothers on how to care for their infants. The company would send a cleaning woman to an employee's home if he or she was facing illness or other difficulties. The Accident Department also provided education to employees on how to avoid job injuries.

To encourage employee identification with the corporation and increase workplace camaraderie, the company created the Amoskeag Textile Club. The idea for the club was inspired by the success of a company-sponsored employee outing to Hampton Beach, New Hampshire, in 1910. The club was incorporated by the State of New Hampshire in 1911 and started out with over four hundred members. It sponsored sporting events and social activities, produced plays and operettas, built a children's playground near the corporation housing area, provided space for a children's garden nearby and published an employee magazine, the *Amoskeag Bulletin*. The club took over the operation of the company's store on Canal Street, which had existed for several years, where employees could purchase Amoskeag fabrics at discounted prices. The proceeds were used to fund the club's activities.

The Amoskeag also created the Amoskeag Textile School, which was affiliated with the Textile Club. Classes were provided for employees who wanted to learn the technical aspects of textile production. Participation in the school's programs was a way for ambitious employees to get ahead within the corporation.

Children in the Amoskeag's playground, viewed looking east across Canal Street, circa 1911. *Manchester Historic Association.*

The Boston Red Sox (on left) and the all-star team from the local Manufacturers' League at Textile Field, September 8, 1913. *Manchester Historic Association.*

In 1912, the Amoskeag turned over control of company-owned Varick Park on Valley Street to the Textile Club. The park included a baseball diamond, a bicycle track and open space for track and field events. The Textile Club replaced the wooden bleachers with a brick and steel grandstand that was designed by the Amoskeag's engineers. The club changed the name of the park to Textile Field (now Gill Stadium). Over fourteen thousand people attended the dedication on September 8, 1913. As described in the 1915 Amoskeag history, "By day the field was alive with games and athletic exercises, and by night resplendent with such a display of fireworks as Manchester has seldom, if ever, witnessed. The star feature of the afternoon was the great ball game between the Boston Red Sox and an all-star team from the local Manufacturers' League."[72] The score was Red Sox 3, All-Stars 1.

With the completion of Mill No. 11 in 1889 and the Coolidge Mill in 1906, the Amoskeag began dealing with the excess land it owned on the west side of Manchester. This land was located to the west of these two mills. In 1902, the company sold land to the city for Lafayette Park for one dollar. In 1912, the company sold Rock Rimmon and about forty-three acres of land around it to the city for one dollar to establish another public park.

The company decided to lay out streets on a grid system on the remainder of its land on the west side and to begin to sell lots for home construction. That same year, the company offered to sell plots of land fifty by one hundred feet in the area between Coolidge Avenue and Rock Rimmon Park to its employees. Any employee who had worked for the company for at least five years could buy a lot by taking a first and second mortgage, each for half the price of the land. The employee would need to build a house on the property within one year. The house could include one or two apartments. The employee would pay no interest on the loan as long as he or she was employed by the company, and after five years, should he or she remain with the company and still be living in the house, the second mortgage could be paid off for one dollar. At the end of ten years, under the same circumstances, the first mortgage could be paid off for a small fee.

By 1915, many lots had been sold to employees. Other lots in that area were sold at market rates to people who were ineligible for the special mortgage program. The neighborhood grew rapidly. Many French-Canadian immigrants settled there, and this section of the west side became known as Little Canada.

With the establishment of a modern, centralized employment system and several high-profile benevolent programs that supported their employees, the Amoskeag projected an aura of great confidence in its future.

Chapter 24
CHILD LABOR

The Amoskeag Manufacturing Company, like other textile firms in New England, employed child workers throughout the nineteenth century and into the twentieth century. Children as young as nine years old were hired to work in the spinning rooms, where their small hands were useful in tying knots when the yarn broke; and in the weave rooms, where they were taught to be doffers (who removed full bobbins of cotton or wool from spinning frames and replaced them with empty ones) or bobbin girls or boys (who carried the full bobbins from the spinning room to the weavers). They were also hired as sweepers and messengers, and teenage boys often worked on construction crews. For many families in Manchester who had come from farming backgrounds in the United States, Canada or Europe, child labor was an accepted fact of life. Children worked on the farms, along with adults, all contributing to the household economy. Why should they not also work in the mills?

Gradually, an awareness developed around the subject of child labor, and opposition to the exploitation of children grew within society. However, for middle-class and lower-middle-class families in Manchester, particularly in the immigrant population, economic necessity continued to drive their decision to send their children to work in the mills.

The National Child Labor Committee (NCLC) was organized in 1904 in New York City at a mass meeting of men and women who were concerned about the lives of working children in America. The organization gained a great deal of support and was chartered by an act

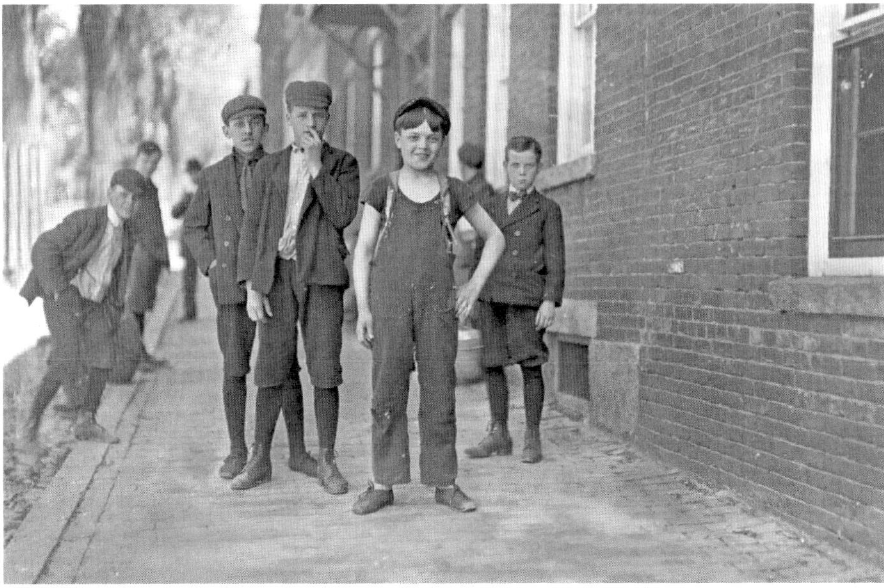

Amoskeag worker Fred Normandin (with bare arms) and friends in corporation housing district. Photograph by Lewis Hine, 1909. *Library of Congress, Prints & Photographs Division, NCLC.*

of Congress in 1907. In 1908, the NCLC hired a New York schoolteacher, Lewis Wickes Hine (1874–1940), as an investigator and documentary photographer to study firsthand the working and living conditions of children. Hine was trained in sociology, and he was deeply worried about the exploitation of children that existed at that time. His poignant images of children in mills, mines, quarries and canneries taken in 1908–09 and 1911–12 were instrumental in raising public awareness regarding child labor and poverty.

Lewis Hine visited Manchester in 1909. He photographed child workers outside the mill yard and was also able to make his way surreptitiously into at least one of the mills so that he could take photographs in the workrooms. Hine conducted brief interviews with some of the children he encountered. He would scribble down their names and other information in his notepad in a way that wouldn't attract attention.

In 1911, under the leadership of New Hampshire's Republican governor, Robert P. Bass of Peterborough, the New Hampshire legislature passed a far-reaching child labor law. This law banned the hiring of children under twelve years old. Children ages twelve and thirteen could only be employed when school was not in session. No prohibitions were included for the hiring of children fourteen years old and older. By 1914, thirty-five states had filed similar legislation.

According to Tamara Hareven:

> *Once the child labor law was in effect, the Amoskeag tried to enforce the age limit by requiring age certificates from young boys and girls. It was, however, fairly easy to bypass this regulation. Often the employment clerk simply asked the age and accepted the answer at face value. Some children did not even stop at the employment office but went directly to the workrooms. If the overseer asked for their age, they simply lied.*[73]

One example illustrates one method of bypassing the law. Valeda Tourigny was born in the province of Quebec, Canada, in 1900. She was one of eleven children of a French-speaking family. The Tourignys arrived in Manchester in 1911 and settled in the Franco-American neighborhood that was developing west of the Coolidge Mill and Mill No. 11. Her father and two brothers found work in the Amoskeag's mill yard where Valeda's brother-in-law, Bert Molloy, was an overseer. To get Valeda a job in the mills, her father obtained a false birth certificate for her in the name of a sister, Cora, who had died as an infant. Valeda used this document when applying for a job at the Amoskeag in 1912, when she was eleven years old. According to the birth certificate that she presented, she was sixteen years old. The company hired her, and for the next several years, she worked primarily as a spinner. Valeda recalled her early days in the mills in an interview for the book *Amoskeag*:

> *When I first started in the Amoskeag, I worked in the spinning room in the Amory Mill. We all worked together. The spinning room was for young girls. We used to dance in the aisles. We'd go in the hallways, and one would watch for the boss while the other one took care of our work. We danced, and a Greek boy played the harmonica. We thought the weave room was for married women and old maids. We had a good time in the spinning room.*[74]

Valeda became known as Cora, and after a while, only her family knew her true name. The Amoskeag's employment office continued to list her age as being older than she really was until she was around nineteen or twenty. Cora began working as a weaver in 1919, and she participated in the strike of 1922. She returned to work late that year. The last slip in her Amoskeag work record shows Cora as working in the Amory Mill as a general helper called a "room girl."[75] She left the mill on August 9, 1935, because the "work run out." Cora married Jules Pellerin in 1931, and the couple had two daughters. Valeda (Cora) (Tourigny) Pellerin died in Manchester in 1993 at the age of ninety-three.

Chapter 25

THE END OF PROSPERITY

The Amoskeag Manufacturing Company reached the height of its glory in the early twentieth century. One young worker, Thomas "Tommy" Smith, an immigrant from Scotland, began his career at the Amoskeag in 1907 as a dyer. He would later become a clerk in the dye house and an assistant supervisor. He described the mill yard circa 1910:

> *Each of the mills had its own bell tower; and when the signal came over the electric wire, the bell ringers would jump onto the ropes. I used to watch them to see how high they could jump. They'd pull the rope down with all their weight. The ropes went up through all the floors to the bell tower, and all the bells would ring. When the bells rang, it was time to go home. The people flocked out of the mills. All the gates on Canal Street would be opened, and the people would come across the bridge. That was something to see. Picture the people coming out of the main gate on Stark Street! They'd be hustling and joking—nine thousand people trying to get out of those gates to get home as quickly as possible. It was fascinating to see! When people heard the bells, they were ready to fly.*[76]

In 1905, the Amoskeag Manufacturing Company bought out the Amory Manufacturing Company and the Manchester Mills. With the purchase of these two large operations, the Amoskeag now owned all the cotton manufacturing facilities in Manchester (with the exception of the Stark Manufacturing Company), and it could now also print its own textiles. Its

One day's production of Amoskeag gingham, date unknown. *Manchester Historic Association.*

reputation as the largest cotton textile–producing plant in the United States seemed to guarantee that it could survive any challenge.

In October 1911, at the same time it was establishing its centralized employment office, the Amoskeag Manufacturing Company underwent a major change in corporate structure. The corporation that was founded in 1831 under the laws of the state of New Hampshire ceased to exist, and all its assets and liabilities were transferred to a new company with the same name. This entity was set up as a "voluntary association," which was essentially a trust. The shareholders of the original corporation became shareholders of the new company. The directors of the original Amoskeag became the new company's trustees. The officers and employees of the original company became the same in the new company. The reason for this change was that, under this arrangement, the trustees had greater autonomy and power than the directors had under the previous business structure.

During this time, the Amoskeag was actively recruiting new employees. In 1912, in conjunction with the Manchester Chamber of Commerce, the company published an illustrated booklet that touted its employment opportunities and listed the benefits that the company provided that were part of the benevolent program instituted the year before.[77] The piece also promoted Manchester as an outstanding place in which to live and do business. The booklet touted Manchester's school system, churches and public parks, plus its central location in New England and its steam railroad, interurban and suburban trolley lines.

The cover was a reproduction of a romantic painting commissioned by the company depicting a Native American at Amoskeag Falls. The publication was illustrated with photographs taken by the Amoskeag's own photography staff. It was produced in both English and French. The French version was used to encourage immigration and trade from Quebec.

The impressive statistics included in the publication show the Amoskeag at its height:

Number of males employed: 8,500
Number of females employed: 7,000
Total number of employees: 15,500

Produces nearly $50,000,000 in manufactured goods annually

Yards of cotton cloth woven per week: 4,715,790
Yards of worsted wool cloth woven per week: 263,640
Total: 4,979,430

Yards of cotton cloth woven per year: 245,221,080
Yards of wool cloth woven per year: 13,709,280
Total: 258,930,360

Miles of cloth woven per hour: 50
Seamless bags woven per year: 1,630,000
Pounds of raw cotton consumed per annum: 54,600,000
Pounds of raw wool consumed per annum: 15,300,000

These statistics seemed overwhelming in proving that there were only good times ahead for the Amoskeag Manufacturing Company and for the textile industry in New England. But the truth was that this company and all the northern textile mills were battling increasing competition from newer mills in the southern United States. Even as the Amoskeag was undertaking tremendous efforts in 1911 to create a more flexible corporate structure and to develop cost-saving efficiencies by establishing a central employment office, and even as it launched an employee welfare program to retain the best workers and to prevent encroachment from labor unions, trouble was on the horizon. In the summer of 1911, several of the Amoskeag's manufacturing departments shut down for several days due to overproduction. The company needed to reduce its inventory, as prices were plummeting in the flooded markets. Similar shutdowns took place in other mills in New England, and as many as thirty-one thousand workers were affected. From 1912 to 1918, there would be times of enormous productivity followed by layoffs, and both wages and work hours became increasingly unstable.

Company production was boosted temporarily during and immediately after World War I as European imports diminished and the country became more dependent on domestic products. Also, the Amoskeag received contracts from the U.S. government for textiles for use in military uniforms. Sales during this time were the highest the Amoskeag had ever experienced. In 1918, the last year of the war, the company made a $7 million profit on sales of $44 million. This, however, marked the end of the era of great prosperity for the Amoskeag Manufacturing Company.

Chapter 26

THE ALL-AMERICAN FLAG

In the early summer of 1914, the Amoskeag Manufacturing Company produced a one-of-a-kind product—a giant American flag. The client was a wealthy Chicago businessman, George Fabyan, who was a principal in the dry goods firm of Bliss, Fabyan & Co. The order had been placed by Fabyan through his friend, the Amoskeag's treasurer, Frederic C. Dumaine.[78]

The forty-eight-star flag was made in the pattern department of Mill No. 11 on the west side of Manchester (now 195 McGregor Street). It was 95 feet long and 50 feet tall and weighed two hundred pounds. Its stars were a yard in diameter and were sewn 4 feet, 9 inches apart. To fly it would have required a flagpole 285 feet tall. However, this flag was not meant to be flown. It was meant to be carried or hung from a building.

The great flag was photographed on June 29, 1914, by Harlan A. Marshall, the chairman of the camera section of the Amoskeag Textile Club. Employees rigged the flag so that it could be hoisted onto the side of Mill No. 11. After it was up, and after Marshall had taken a few preliminary shots, over one hundred employees from the mill stopped work so they could pose in front of the flag. Marshall turned the photos he took that day into lantern slides, which were shown during the Fourth of July week in a downtown theater. The audiences applauded wildly. The Amoskeag's employees could purchase an eight- by ten-inch copy of the photo for forty-five cents by applying directly to Marshall.

According to the Amoskeag employee newsletter, the *Amoskeag Bulletin*, of July 1, 1914, "The bunting of which it [the flag] is constructed was

The "All-American Flag" made by the Amoskeag Manufacturing Company in 1914. *Manchester Historic Association.*

specially manufactured for the purpose. Amoskeag spun, Amoskeag woven, Amoskeag dyed and Amoskeag constructed—an All-American Flag!"[79]

The flag was shipped to George Fabyan in Chicago. Fabyan brought it to St. Louis, Missouri, where it was carried in a parade. He then sold it to Marshall Field & Company, the famous Chicago department store. In 1916, F.C. Dumaine asked the store if he could borrow it for a few days. The store shipped the flag to Dumaine at his New York office. It was featured at the head of the Citizens Preparedness Parade on May 13, 1916. During the parade, 70 men from two prominent New York dry goods companies carried it down the streets of the city. The flag was preceded by the Seventh Regiment band and followed close behind by three groups of employees from the New York selling offices of the Amoskeag Manufacturing Company. The march lasted for twelve hours and involved an estimated 175,000 people. The flag was shipped back to Marshall Field's immediately after the parade so that the store could display it in its atrium on Memorial Day and the Fourth of July.

The New York parade was one of many that were held in major cities beginning in 1914 as part of the Preparedness Movement, which was a populist effort to urge the U.S. government to prepare for the country's potential involvement in the war that was raging in Europe. American flags figured prominently as a motif in these parades. One of the leaders of the movement was former U.S. president Theodore Roosevelt.

The ultimate fate of the flag is unknown, but its image, with the lineup of proud millworkers standing in front of it, remains. The photograph was published in *National Geographic* magazine in October 1917 in a special edition devoted to flags. The publication was distributed free to thousands of American servicemen who were preparing to depart for Europe to fight in World War I. The image has been reproduced countless times in history texts and in magazines and has also appeared on film. It evokes a feeling of patriotism, as well as pride in the contributions of labor in a free society. For those who know Manchester and the multi-ethnic makeup of the Amoskeag workforce, the photograph tells the story of hardworking and hopeful immigrants who were taking part in the great work of the American manufacturing industry.

Chapter 27

THE STRIKE OF 1922

Prior to 1922, the Amoskeag Manufacturing Company experienced only occasional labor agitation. The most notable and serious of these occurrences took place in 1855. In 1854, the workday at several textile mills in Manchester was reduced from eleven and three-quarters hours to eleven, but management reinstituted the original length of the workday in early 1855. As told by scholar James P. Hanlan, on one morning in March 1855, several hundred female workers of the Manchester Print Works

> *took to parading in the streets. They were joined, after lunch, by large numbers from other mills—the Stark and Amoskeag—who responded to the bell calling them back from lunch by taking to the streets. Led by a band, the workers marched through the streets of Manchester, carrying banners, cheering, and singing. Mass meetings were held on that first afternoon and the evening as well as on the next day. Some of the town's prominent middle-class business leaders and politicians acted as go-between, carrying communications and information between* [the mill] *agents and workers. The only response which workers consistently drew from agents was that they should "adhere to their regulations."*[80]

The strikers met with the new mayor of Manchester, Theodore T. Abbott, who was a firm supporter of the mill managers and was angered by the audacity of the workers. The strikers' band interrupted him whenever he tried to speak. One of the protesters, a mechanic, reached into his dinner

The Amoskeag Manufacturing Company employment office at 387 Canal Street, circa 1920. *Manchester Historic Association.*

The first parade of strikers on April 10, 1922, shown crossing the McGregor Bridge from the east side of the Merrimack River. *Manchester Historic Association.*

pail and threw his lunch at the mayor. It was reported that a donut struck the head of the agent of the Manchester Print Works.

The workers marched every day for three weeks, gathering sympathy from the local citizens, as well as donations. The Manchester Print Works and the Stark Manufacturing Company were closed down, but the Amoskeag continued running, though only barely. Two young women were assaulted by mill officials when they tried to collect their back pay. As support for the strikers grew in the community, their opponents became quiet. The strikers never reached a formal settlement with the managers, but they were assured indirectly that the eleven-hour workday would be reinstated, which it eventually was. Workers returned to their jobs in April, but many left Manchester for jobs in other cities. The three companies were left with a labor shortage.

The subject of the reduction of work hours in order to provide workers with the opportunity to lead more healthful and balanced lives was the focus of what was known as the Ten-Hour Movement. This effort had started in the 1830s among workers in the quarries, textile mills and other trades and continued well into the twentieth century. It is interesting to note that New Hampshire became the first state to institute a ten-hour workday law in 1847, and Pennsylvania followed in 1848. These laws were essentially ineffective, as both states had included a clause that allowed an employee to voluntarily agree to work more than ten hours a day. Virtually all employees were deemed to have voluntarily agreed to work the long hours that the employers mandated, either implicitly by accepting the position or explicitly by signing a contract.

There were a few incidents of labor unrest at the Amoskeag in the 1880s, including an eighteen-day strike of gingham weavers in February 1886. The Knights of Labor union became involved in the settlement, but this union would have a short-lived presence in Manchester. Attempts by this and other unions to gain a foothold in the mill yard were rebuffed by employees.

Minor walkouts occurred in 1912, 1913 and 1914. This was a sign of employee discontent that existed during a time when the company was working to find ways to reduce labor costs while still maintaining good working relationships between labor and management. But the Amoskeag was not immune to the strains that were being felt throughout the textile industry.

The United Textile Workers (UTW) union was finally able to establish a presence in the mill yard in 1917. In June 1918, the union organized a strike to demand a pay increase of 15 percent instead of the 12 percent that the Amoskeag had planned to give. The Amoskeag mills were mostly producing textiles under contract with the U.S. government at the time due to the U.S. involvement in World War I. A government arbitrator was sent from Washington, D.C., to persuade the company to consent to the 15 percent pay raise. It did, and the strike was ended within just five days.

The gradual decline in the textile industry in New England, which had begun toward the end of the nineteenth century, was forestalled for a few years by the effects of World War I (1914–18). When the war ended in 1918, the government contracts awarded to the Amoskeag Manufacturing Company ended also. However, for the next several months, the demand for Amoskeag goods still held up. This favorable situation was over by the end of 1921, as European production of textiles was restarted. The Amoskeag and the entire American textile industry was in trouble, particularly the northern mills. It was a case of overproduction combined with a reduction in demand. One of the factors that impacted the Amoskeag greatly was the change in clothing styles. Women's fashions now favored clothing with less fabric, and cotton was being displaced by other types of cloth, including silk and artificial silk (rayon and similar fabrics). The modern woman was less likely to wear a gingham dress.

The *Springfield Leader* newspaper of Springfield, Illinois, published a large advertisement for the local Reps Dry Goods Co. store on March 12, 1922. The store was promoting a sale of fifteen thousand yards of Amoskeag gingham remnants at cut-rate prices. The ad read, "We are proud of this honor for it *is* an honor, to be chosen as the store through which this merchandise passes. We are proud and glad that we are able to offer these, the standard of all ginghams, to our customers at prices lower, in most cases, than other stores must ask for material of ordinary character, for Amoskeag is truly the last word in gingham perfection."[81] Although the Amoskeag's textiles were highly regarded, the economic signs were clear that the corporation needed to make changes in the way it was operating if there was to be any hope of it remaining viable. Retail discounts meant that the wholesalers also were paying less for the product, so the Amoskeag's profit margins were plunging.

The Amoskeag dealt with this situation, in part, by reducing the wages of its employees while increasing hours. On February 2, 1922, an announcement from the Amoskeag's agent, William Parker Straw, was posted throughout the mill yard: "Commencing Monday, Feb. 13, 1922, a reduction of 20 per cent will be made in all hour and piece rates in all departments of the Amoskeag. At the same time the running time of the mills will be increased from 48 to 54 hours per week in accordance with the schedule posted herewith."[82]

From the viewpoint of treasurer F.C. Dumaine, these measures were necessary to maintain some level of profitability. Later in 1922, he wrote, "It is not a new thing that has come suddenly upon New England. It is a menace that had been steadily growing since the extreme pressure of demand caused by the war ceased. To operate the Amoskeag Mills at a loss could have but one result. In a short time they would be closed."[83]

The managers of the Stark Manufacturing Company adopted the same policy. Approximately fifteen thousand Amoskeag employees and two thousand workers at the Stark Manufacturing Company were affected. Even with the increase in hours, the employees would be taking home less money in their pay envelopes. This reduction in pay was difficult to accept, but the increase in work hours was unbearable.

The pay reduction and lengthening of hours led to a nine-month strike of the Amoskeag's and the Stark's workers that was led by the United Textile Workers. The strike began on February 13, 1922. During the course of the strike, officials from the UTW, Protestant clergy organizations, Roman Catholic bishop George Albert Guertin and New Hampshire labor commissioner John S.B. Davie all approached the officers of the Amoskeag Manufacturing Company on behalf of the strikers, but to no avail. The workers appealed to New Hampshire governor Albert O. Brown and to the New Hampshire legislature to enact a forty-eight-hour workweek law. This attempt also failed.

The strikers began to picket, and the first mass meetings of workers in Manchester's history took place at the Palace and the Park Theatres on February 20. According to Hareven:

> *During the first two months of the strike, as picketing continued along the mill yard, union leaders and the strike committee organized mass meetings, rallies, and parades to boost strikers' morale. Strikers sold tags and roses in the streets to raise funds for the strike. On March 13, Samuel Gompers, president of the American Federation of Labor, addressed a mass meeting, urging the strikers "to fight to the end no matter what the consequences may be."*[84]

On June 2, 1922, the Amoskeag acquired the Stark Manufacturing Company from its then owner, the International Cotton Mills. Ironically, in 1839, the Stark Manufacturing Company was the first textile company to operate in the mill yard, and in the end, it was the last textile company in the mill yard to be taken over by the Amoskeag.

From the beginning of the strike, a small number of workers refused to participate. This enabled the Amoskeag to restart a few of its manufacturing rooms in early April 1922. The strike proceeded without the threat of violence against these operatives. However, by late spring, tensions were mounting. On June 1, the Amoskeag announced that it planned to open the Coolidge Mill in west Manchester and to employ anyone who wanted work. The UTW and the strikers saw this decision as an affront, as the company was now publicizing that it would rehire strikers who were willing to come back and that it would hire new workers to replace the strikers.

On the day of the Coolidge's opening, June 5, people began to congregate outside the mill gates at the northeast corner of McGregor and West Bridge Streets at about 4:00 a.m. Chief of Police M.J. Healy had assigned every available Manchester police officer to be on duty. The company's official account of what happened read:

> *Many who undoubtedly came to the plant with the intention of seeking their former jobs decided to remain outside rather than face the hostile crowd. According to union officials 127 people, including overseers, second hands and clerks entered the gates leading to the Coolidge…Police officers could do little but keep the mass of people moving slowly up and down West Bridge, McGregor and Amory streets as the hour for the opening of the Coolidge approached…At 6 o'clock a male operative went to the gate and waited for it to open. He was followed by others in pairs and in a comparatively short time more than 100 had entered…It was quite apparent to the neutral observer that a number of the operatives in the mass came with the intention of working. They were evidently scared by the thousands lined up outside the gate and remained away from the looms.*[85]

Two people were arrested—Frank A. Foye, son of police sergeant William Foye, and David J. McIntire—and "were later released after a warning lecture by police authorities."[86]

Matters got worse at 5:30 p.m., when the workday ended at the Coolidge Mill:

> *As the closing hour drew near people began to hurry across the bridge to be present when the workers left the mill. They were met at the foot of West Bridge Street by policemen who cautioned them to keep moving. The line increased in numbers until 5:15 o'clock one side of the highway was banked solid with humanity. At 5:30 o'clock the buzz of machinery stopped. The*

> *main gate was thrown open and as if by signal the paraders faced the mill. Vainly the officers tried to start the procession moving. They were unable to budge the crowd. The first worker came out of the building and started for the gate. A roar went up and he hurried down the street accompanied by the jeers of the strikers.*[87]

The taunts continued as other workers left the Coolidge Mill, and by 6:00 p.m., the mill's gates were closed and the two thousand people who had assembled there went home. The angry crowd was even larger the next morning. The agitated strikers and their sympathizers were forced to remain on the opposite side of West Bridge Street from the mill, where they loudly heckled the workers as they entered the building. Later in the morning, some strikers scuffled with police, including a few who protested near the police station downtown. In total, the police arrested fifteen local strikers for inciting to riot and disorderly conduct. When four UTW officials showed up at the police station to inquire about the people under custody, they were also arrested. These included the strike organizer, Horace A. Riviere.

The local strikers were fined from $5.82 to $10.00 for their role in the disturbance. The union officials were released on $1,000.00 bonds. Horace Riviere, UTW vice-president James Starr (who had not been involved in the previous day's events) and other union officials met with Chief Healy at the police station. After the meeting, Starr announced to reporters, "We have told Chief Healy that we will cooperate so far as is humanly possible to keep the peace."[88]

The union kept its word. On the third day of work at the Coolidge Mill, the strikers, now in fewer numbers, held a silent demonstration. Afterward, the union was forced to stop any picketing in Manchester as the Amoskeag Manufacturing Company had managed to obtain an injunction against public demonstrations. Some of the people working at the Coolidge Mill were harassed outside the area of the mill, including one man who was pelted with stones while walking home. At the end of July, the strikers were allowed to station two picketers at each mill gate.

The Coolidge Mill kept operating, and by Labor Day, about 2,500 Amoskeag workers had either gone back to work or hadn't left in the first place. As the weeks wore on, the company hired more people and began to restart more departments. On November 14, the company reported that twenty mills were operating.

The problems between millworkers and management were, of course, not limited to Manchester. The year 1922 saw strikes in all the leading textile centers in New Hampshire, Rhode Island and Massachusetts (with the exception of New Bedford and Fall River). Wage and hour issues were foremost in the minds of the strikers, but the specific reasons for the strikes varied from city to city. In total, about sixty thousand workers were affected.

The Manchester walkout was the last New England strike to be settled. The UTW called off the strike on November 26, 1922, and the workers returned to work on November 27. The wage scales of the employees were restored to pre-strike levels, but the increase in hours remained. The workers would now face fifty-four-hour workweeks, versus the forty-eight hours they had worked before. The bitter experience of the strike resulted in the UTW having little influence among workers in Manchester for the next ten years.

The strike of 1922 resulted in distressed situations for many people in Manchester. The city's strikers lost about $11 million in wages and also lost many of the benefits that the Amoskeag once provided to them. Nearly every person in the city was either directly affected or had a family member who was. Families were split apart, some by discord about whether or not to participate in the strike and some when family members had to leave the city to find work elsewhere in New England or Canada.

The Great Depression (1929–39) was years away, but for Manchester and other New England textile cities, the Depression began in 1922. Manchester certainly had other industries, notably shoe manufacturing and cigar making, but the Amoskeag Manufacturing Company was then, as it had been throughout its history, the largest employer in town. Its decline affected everyone.

In the years following the 1922 strikes, relations between labor and management became increasingly strained within the textile industry. Deteriorating work conditions, including work speedups and low wages, led to widespread employee dissatisfaction. In March 1933, the Amoskeag reduced its wages. The employees initially accepted the situation, but anger grew, and on May 19, about eight thousand workers went on strike. The company announced that it would shut down operations until August 1 and afterward give the employees a 15 percent raise. The purpose of the shutdown was to sell off its excess inventories, which would justify restarting the mills in August to replenish stock. A week after the strike started, four thousand strikers, working with the UTW, crowded the company's main gate at the foot of Stark Street. Four units of the New Hampshire National Guard were called out to keep order. When the guardsmen arrived at the State Armory on Canal Street, about two thousand strikers threw rocks at them. Seventy people were injured and thirty-nine strikers arrested.

On September 1, 1934, an estimated 500,000 textile workers in the United States went on strike, led by the UTW. In New England, 160,000 workers joined the strike, including employees of the Amoskeag Manufacturing Company. The local textile workforce of around 8,500 people was affected. After three weeks, the strike collapsed, and the mills in Manchester were reopened on September 21. The employees lost $360,000 in wages, and the Amoskeag lost business.

Chapter 28

BANKRUPTCY

After the strike of 1922, the Amoskeag needed to get back to business, but it wouldn't be business as usual. By this time, the competition created by the existence of the new southern mills accelerated. The new mills operated more efficiently than the antiquated plants in the North. They were close to the sources of cotton, which reduced shipping costs, and they were geared up for producing modern textiles, which had been a slow and uneven process in the North. With these new mills operating and the northern mills continuing to make cloth, overproduction created gluts in the market, especially for cotton textiles. For the Amoskeag, as for all the northern textile companies, the competition for market share was a constant preoccupation, as was deflation in the selling price of the cotton goods that were flooding the market.

The Amoskeag's investors understood that the viability of the company was not a certainty, and the decision was made to reshape the corporate structure to protect assets. In 1925, the Amoskeag Manufacturing Company trust (created in 1911) was transformed into a holding company called the Amoskeag Company, and a new trust was formed to continue the manufacturing and related functions in Manchester. This trust was given the name Amoskeag Manufacturing Company. It retained the buildings, equipment and other real assets of the 1911 Amoskeag Manufacturing Company trust, plus $6 million in cash. The remaining cash plus investments of the 1911 trust remained with the new holding company. This amounted to assets of around $18 million. The Amoskeag Company became the parent

Frederic C. Dumaine, treasurer of the Amoskeag Manufacturing Company, 1916. *Manchester Historic Association.*

corporation (essentially the owner) of the "new" Amoskeag Manufacturing Company.

This left the manufacturing operation with limited funding and outdated equipment and buildings. The situation was compounded in 1926 when the Amoskeag Manufacturing Company was recapitalized, which resulted in a payoff to some of the investors in the holding company and a reduction in the money available to support the manufacturing operations. The Amoskeag attempted to become more profitable by increasing the efficiency of its operations. The company bought some new equipment and sold off surplus real estate. It cut back on benefits and laid off employees. Those who remained had to speed up their work.

In 1925, the Amoskeag acquired the Parkhill Manufacturing Company of Fitchburg, Massachusetts, so that it could control this major competitor in the gingham market. Also, the Amoskeag now had access to Parkhill's cotton plantations in Arkansas, which provided the company with an inexpensive and reliable source of cotton. Another benefit of gaining control of this company was that Parkhill was also engaged in rayon production. This gave the Amoskeag a foothold in this industry at a time when rayon was gaining popularity in the fashion industry. The Amoskeag's venture in the rayon business didn't succeed very well, however, as the company was faced with inadequate equipment and other problems. The Amoskeag abandoned this line of business in 1933.

Between 1929 and 1935, the Amoskeag Manufacturing Company suffered a total deficit of $5 million. With the company's various attempts to remain profitable eventually failing, treasurer Frederic C. Dumaine and the investors decided that the corporation could not continue operating under the old business model. In September 1935, the Amoskeag Manufacturing Company closed its doors, and for the first time, the entire mill yard was quiet.

In early March 1935, the Amoskeag employed 11,014 workers. At the end of June, the number was down to 6,000. There were more layoffs, so by the time the mills closed in September, there were only 1,000 people employed. That year, 6,272 Amoskeag workers registered with the state unemployment office. In November 1935, 22.8 percent of Manchester's families were on welfare. About one-quarter of former Amoskeag employees left the city in desperation to look for work.

The Amoskeag Manufacturing Company filed for bankruptcy on Christmas Eve 1935. That day, the headline in the late edition of the *Manchester Leader and Evening Union* newspaper read, "Amoskeag Moves to Reorganize." The article explained that the first step had been taken under the federal bankruptcy act in the federal court in Boston to reorganize the company to "make operations profitable." The intention of the company's managers was to "open such mills as may be run at a profit and to sell or lease the other mills." The article explained that "committees of the bondholders and the stockholders will be named to cooperate with the trustees in 'selling' the proposition of reorganization to those holding millions in Amoskeag securities. Once this is accomplished, the question of refinancing can be more easily handled by the courts and all affairs expedited."[89] The mills in Manchester would remain closed, but at least there was a glimmer of hope that the company would reopen in 1936, though on a much smaller scale than before.

In the coming weeks, the Amoskeag, led by treasurer F.C. Dumaine, began working through the process of reorganization and refinancing. It is uncertain if this plan would have eventually succeeded, but the efforts were dealt a heavy blow through an act of nature. In March 1936, the Amoskeag Manufacturing Company sustained $2.5 million in damage due to the worst flood that had ever affected the Merrimack River in recorded history. It would have been impossible for the Amoskeag to reinvent itself without a large influx of cash, and the investors in the holding company were unwilling to invest in the company.

The Roman Catholic bishop of Manchester, Reverend John B. Peterson, pleaded in person with the Amoskeag investors to forget dollars and cents and think about the human element. The stockholders simply did not want to put additional cash into the company to try to keep it afloat when there were so many factors weighing against the possibility of success.

The Amoskeag's workers had voted to accept wage reductions to help the company reopen, and the City of Manchester had recently provided the company with tax relief by reassessing the value of its property from $13 million down to $6,750,000. But that wasn't enough.

The decision delivered by federal judge George C. Sweeney on July 21, 1936, per recommendation of the federal referee in bankruptcy, Arthur Black, was that the Amoskeag Manufacturing Company be liquidated. The company's attorney was prepared to accept this decision on behalf of the investors. The Amoskeag's assets were set to be sold at auction. At this time, there were two thousand families and five hundred individuals in Manchester on county and city relief out of a population of seventy thousand. The relief agencies estimated that about half the welfare recipients were former Amoskeag employees.

When the news came that the corporation would not be able to make a comeback and the mill yard may well be left empty, most people in Manchester were distressed. The majority of Manchester's citizens had so closely identified with the Amoskeag Manufacturing Company for so many years that they felt a sense of abandonment, betrayal and loss. Local historian and former mayor John C. Mongan wrote in 1993:

> *Before the operating company was dissolved, it paid off all creditors and all bond holders—the holding company recovered every cent but the employees got nothing, no severance, nothing. The bitterness lasted their lifetimes. The idea of "family" had been a hoax. William Parker Straw resigned as agent before the end because he wanted no part in what was taking place. Viewed from today's context, it would appear that closings do happen and owners do take their money out to apply elsewhere. But the Amoskeag employees had a different view—they had lost their livelihood while the owners lost nothing—there was a 100-year company obligation to the employees to modernize, become efficient and remain open. Probably that debate here and elsewhere will never end.*[90]

There were some people in Manchester, however, who saw the situation in a different light. They were grateful that the city's fortunes would no longer be tied to the fate of one large corporation. To them, the dissolution of the Amoskeag Manufacturing Company presented an unprecedented opportunity to reshape Manchester.

Chapter 29

AMOSKEAG INDUSTRIES

Reinventing the Mill Yard

At the end of August 1936, it was announced that the auction of Amoskeag Manufacturing Company assets (including mill buildings, machinery, workers' housing and other real estate) was scheduled for October 21. Several foreign investors planned to gut the buildings and ship the textile machinery overseas. The mill yard would be turned into a ghost town, with many buildings left empty. Fortunately, there was a group of influential people in the city who ignored this potential scenario of doom and gloom. What they saw instead was eight million square feet of space ready to be fitted up for new occupancy and an intact power system that included water power canals, a hydroelectric plant and steam plants. They also saw a workforce eager for jobs.

At around the time that the auction date was announced, Avery Schiller of Public Service Company of New Hampshire; financier Frank P. Carpenter; former mayor Arthur Moreau; Attorney John McLane; Edmund Jewel, publisher of the *Manchester Leader and Evening Union*; and other local leaders got together and formed the Manchester Citizens' Committee on Amoskeag Affairs, which had as its purpose the rehabilitation of the mill yard.

The committee didn't miss a beat. On August 10, the group published a booklet entitled *The Truth about Manchester*, which contained solid facts and figures that touted Manchester's many assets. The introductory paragraphs read:

> *The City of Manchester, N.H., has received a great deal of notice in the metropolitan press since the announcement of the decision to liquidate*

> *the Amoskeag Manufacturing Co. A great deal of misinformation is being circulated...to the effect that Manchester is in a severe sinking spell, that it cannot recover from the shock of the closing of the mills and that conditions here are in a terrible state...Manchester is not down and out. In fact, conditions here are generally better than they were during the first 6 months of 1935 when the Amoskeag Mills were running. This is not a mere statement of a personal opinion but is based on actual information received by means of direct contact with some of the seventy-four heads of various businesses and industrial organizations representing a cross section of the city's economic life... The importance of Manchester as a trade center is sometimes lost sight of because it has long been thought of just as a textile manufacturing center.*[91]

The publication explained that, from 1930 to 1936, Manchester's population had increased from 76,834 to nearly 79,000 and that it had a significant manufacturing base that included rayon and wool textiles, cigars, shoes, furniture, food, brushes, coffins, paper, felt hats and soap. Manchester's other businesses included farming, recreational activities, retail, banking, utilities and insurance. Many individual businesses were reporting increased profits from a year before, and the number of people on welfare was declining. The document contained exhaustive factual details to back up its claims.

The committee members needed to find a way to take control of the situation. They asked the bankruptcy referee, Arthur Black, how they could stop the auction and acquire the assets of the Amoskeag outright. He answered that the price would be $5 million (this was the appraisal value of the property set by the liquidating trustees) and that he would require a $500,000 down payment, in cash, within ten days.

On September 2, 1936, this group and other Manchester leaders chartered a new corporation, Amoskeag Industries, Inc., with Arthur Moreau as president. The other officers were John R. McLane, clerk; Frank P. Carpenter, vice-president; and local businessman Willard D. Rand, treasurer. William Parker Straw, the former agent of the Amoskeag Manufacturing Company, became the agent of the new corporation. On September 3, a certified check for $500,000 was delivered to the liquidating trustees in Boston by Arthur Moreau, Harry L. Davis and several other representatives of Amoskeag Industries. Federal referee Black agreed to postpone the auction from October 14 to October 21.

On September 15, the court approved the sale of the assets to Amoskeag Industries, which now had to raise $4.5 million to complete the deal. This was quickly accomplished. Public Service Company of New Hampshire, an electrical utility that served Manchester and southern and western New Hampshire, provided nearly half the money needed by buying the Amoskeag's hydroelectric plant for $2.25 million, and it also purchased $100,000 in shares in the new company. The remainder of the money was raised from five local banks and through the sale of stock to local financiers. In 1937, Public Service purchased the Northern Division Power House, further investing in the success of the new company.[92]

Amoskeag Industries became the sole owner of the assets of the Amoskeag Manufacturing Company. This included the mill yard, which contained 104 buildings, two canals, machinery, tools and vehicles. Amoskeag Industries also took ownership of 106 workers' housing units, plus other real estate in Manchester, and was awarded reverter rights to churches, schools and parks that had been built on former Amoskeag lands.

The main purpose of Amoskeag Industries was simple—to attract diversified industries to the city so that Manchester would no longer have to depend on one company or one type of industry to fuel its economy. As soon as the transaction was completed, Amoskeag Industries began advertising to attract new employers to the city. This brought favorable attention to Manchester. The headline of an article in the *Boston Traveler* newspaper on January 9, 1937, said it all: "Death of Amoskeag Blessing."[93] This was a rare success story in the midst of the Great Depression. Manchester's achievement in pulling itself up by its bootstraps made national news. In 1937, a six-minute documentary-style film was shot in the city. Local citizens, including several of the founders of Amoskeag Industries, portrayed themselves in a dramatized reenactment of the events of 1935 and 1936. This compelling *March of Time* newsreel, entitled *Amoskeag—Success Story*, was shown in movie theaters throughout the country. This was the era before television, so these well-produced short films were very popular as a way to see what was going on in the world.

The newsreel inspired people across the country. For example, the *Evening Times* newspaper of Sayre, Pennsylvania, on December 2, 1937, publicized a special showing that was to take place in Athens, Pennsylvania, the next day:

> *Valley businessmen will be given a dramatic demonstration of the value of cooperation for community welfare tomorrow afternoon at 1:30 o'clock when they will view a* March of Time *film at the Morley theatre in*

> *Athens as guests of the Valley alliance. All business men of the valley are invited to attend the showing, which will be free and will last about a half an hour. The picture shows what happened when a group of business men, refusing to accept defeat, saved Manchester, N.H. from industrial paralysis when the great American cotton mills went into bankruptcy... Today Manchester is back on the map of industry. Smoke hangs in the air along the Merrimack River.*[94]

One of the first companies to move into a former Amoskeag mill was the Chicopee Manufacturing Company, a subsidiary of Johnson & Johnson, which took over the Coolidge Mill on the west side of the Merrimack. It used the existing Amoskeag equipment to manufacture cotton gauze. By March 1938, about 5 million square feet of mill yard space was already occupied by manufacturers, service businesses and warehouses. "Still, the job is not completed," Amoskeag Industries reported in a special edition of the *Union* newspaper, "for 3,000,000 square feet of unusually fine manufacturing floor space is yet idle, and until the bulk of this is sold, or leased, the job will not be finished...valuable mills are awaiting tenants who seek the advantages of Manchester's plentiful skilled help, low cost power, advantageous laws and taxes, accessibility to market and raw materials."[95]

Within eighteen months of its founding, Amoskeag Industries had attracted thirty-nine additional companies to the mill yard. With its newly diversified industrial base, Manchester was ready to do its part for the war production effort in World War II, including producing life preservers, electronic components and rayon for parachutes.

By the 1950s, there were over 75 different businesses operating in the revitalized mill yard. By 1961, Amoskeag Industries had sold all of the former Amoskeag Manufacturing Company assets, and the mill yard housed 132 different businesses. In addition to the Chicopee Manufacturing Company, several of the larger corporations operating in the mill yard would provide employment for hundreds of people for many years. Among these were Arms Textile Manufacturing Co. (textiles); Anchor Manufacturing Company (metal stampings); J.F. McElwain Company (shoes); Silver Brothers Company, Inc. (bottlers); W.M. Auclair (trucking); Waumbec Mills, Inc. (textiles); Chicopee Manufacturing Company (textiles); Textron, Incorporated (textiles); Manchester Knitted Fashions, Inc. (knitted goods); and Pandora Industries (knitted goods).

Amoskeag Industries accomplished its purpose admirably, saving Manchester from a dreary fate. The company continues to exist today as a positive force in the city.

Chapter 30

POSTSCRIPT

From 1969 into the late 1970s, the Amoskeag Manufacturing Company's mill yard was transformed, and not without considerable controversy. By that time, the manufacturing industry had largely left the city during a general period of decline in U.S. manufacturing. Although a few firms still had plants in Manchester, there was increasing impetus to move these operations into modern quarters in the suburbs. Manchester needed to reinvent itself, so it embarked on an urban renewal initiative that had far-reaching consequences. A big part of the process was dealing with the deteriorating and obsolete mill yard, which could not be resurrected in the form in which it had existed. The big question then was whether or not to tear down the mill yard and start over. The bitter memories of the strike of 1922 and the shutdown and bankruptcy of 1935–36 were still fresh in people's minds and hearts. In the end, the decision was made to keep the mill yard but to reshape it for modern use. About half of the buildings were torn down, parking lots were built and the canals were buried. The main railroad track along Canal Street was moved on top of the buried Upper Canal, and the path of the buried Lower Canal became Commercial Street. These and other changes led to a renaissance for the mill yard and for Manchester that continues today.

The Amoskeag Manufacturing Company's legacy includes the magnificent Amoskeag Millyard, as it is known today. Each of the remaining mill buildings stands out for its massive structure, built to last centuries, and for its uniqueness of detail. A wide variety of businesses call the Amoskeag Millyard their home,

Left: The Mill Girl statue located next to the southwest corner of the Stark Mill, created by sculptor Antoinette Schultze in 1988. *Photographed by the author.*

Below: A portion of the Amoskeag Millyard, looking west over the Bridge Street Bridge, February 2015. *Photographed by the author.*

including high-technology and engineering firms that are carrying on with the Amoskeag's can-do tradition of innovation. The University of New Hampshire's urban campus is housed there, and hundreds of people now live in loft apartments in the Millyard. The Merrimack River and Amoskeag Falls link the Millyard to the natural world in an immediate and vital way. The former corporation housing district is considered to be the most intact collection of nineteenth-century workers' housing in the United States and is widely admired. These charming buildings on tree-lined streets are filled with offices, apartments and condominiums.

The clock tower of the Jefferson Mill, April 2014. *Photographed by the author.*

The city's streetscape, public parks and arrangement of neighborhoods are all part of the Amoskeag's legacy. In fact, the very existence of Manchester as a city is the result of the Amoskeag's planning and its long-term stewardship of its vision for the city. Today, descendants of the Amoskeag's workers are still a big part of Manchester's population and are influential in its leadership. The Amoskeag's legacy also includes the rich history it created that is continuously being rediscovered and reinterpreted. It is a history of contrasts that includes both the triumphs and failures of big enterprise and the intimate stories of the company's employees. The Amoskeag Manufacturing Company's story is the story of America.

Today, the Manchester Historic Association works to preserve the history of the Amoskeag Manufacturing Company and the city of Manchester. The association, founded in 1929, makes its archival materials available to the public at its Research Center at 129 Amherst Street in Manchester. The organization houses the records of the Amoskeag Manufacturing Company, including hundreds of photographs taken by the Amoskeag's

The Elm Street Gallery in the Millyard Museum. *Manchester Historic Association.*

own photographers, plus engineering drawings, ledger books, employment records, and many other materials related to the company.[96] Its vast photography collection is accessible for viewing online. The association also operates the Millyard Museum, located at 200 Bedford Street in the Amoskeag Millyard (Mill No. 3). This facility occupies mill space that once held two hundred looms for weaving cotton textiles. The museum contains the only penstock still visible in the mill yard and many informative and beautiful exhibits about the history of Manchester, with a strong focus on the story of the Amoskeag Manufacturing Company and its workers. For further information, visit www.manchesterhistoric.org.

The historical preservation of the Amoskeag Millyard and the Amoskeag Corporation Housing Historic District is overseen by the City of Manchester's Heritage Commission. For information, visit www.manchesternh.gov.

NOTES

Preface

1. The former mill yard of the Amoskeag Manufacturing Company is today known as the Amoskeag Millyard. The spelling of "mill yard" as "millyard" seems to be unique, or nearly unique, to its modern use in reference to the remnants of the industrial plant developed by the Amoskeag Manufacturing Company in Manchester, New Hampshire. Because the compound word "millyard" is not found in dictionaries, it is only used in this book when referring to the Amoskeag Millyard and when the word "millyard" is used in a quotation. Also, the Amoskeag Manufacturing Company as well as individual buildings in the mill yard have often been referred to as the Manchester Mills. As the Manchester Mills existed in the Amoskeag's mill yard as a separate company from the Amoskeag Manufacturing Company, the term "Manchester Mills" is only used when referring to that specific company.

Chapter 2

2. Potter, *History of Manchester*, 45.
3. John Stark of Derryfield (1728–1822) grew up at his family's home near the east bank of the Merrimack River, overlooking Amoskeag Falls. This property was acquired by the Amoskeag Manufacturing Company in the 1830s. Stark was a captain in Rogers Rangers during the French and Indian War in the 1750s, serving under Major Robert Rogers. He is known as the victorious commander of the colonial troops at the Battle of Bennington (1777) during the American Revolution, and he later rose to

the rank of major general in the Continental army. In civilian life, Stark was a lumberman and farmer.

4. Samuel Blodget (or Blodgett, 1724–1807) was a merchant, lumberman, farmer, industrialist and inventor who lived in Haverhill, Massachusetts, and in Goffstown and Derryfield, New Hampshire. He faced many difficulties in building and financing his transportation canal at Amoskeag Falls.
5. A wing dam is a barrier built partway into a river that deflects water in a particular direction. This water could be used to power water wheels for saw, grist and other types of mills or for providing water for transportation or water power canals.
6. Browne, *Amoskeag Manufacturing Co.*, 25.

Chapter 3

7. Ibid., 30.

Chapter 4

8. John Stark Jr. was the son of Major General John Stark.
9. This farm had been settled by Robert McGregor (1749–1816), the son of the Reverend David McGregor (1710–1777), who led the settlement of Nutfield by the Scots-Irish in 1719.
10. Browne, *Amoskeag Manufacturing Co.*, 45.
11. In textile manufacturing in the nineteenth century, the agent's position was similar to that of a chief operating officer of a modern corporation. The agent, acting under the direction of the company's officers, was the senior on-site manager responsible for the company's day-to-day operations.
12. Browne, *Amoskeag Manufacturing Co.*, 47.

Chapter 5

13. Amoskeag Village was part of the town of Goffstown until 1853, when it, along with Piscataquog Village to its south, was annexed by Manchester.
14. Browne, *Amoskeag Manufacturing Co.*, 49.
15. Oliver Dean papers, Manchester Historic Association.
16. Browne, *Amoskeag Manufacturing Co.*, 47.
17. The first bridge over Amoskeag Falls was built in 1842. It was destroyed in a freshet in 1853, and a covered bridge was built to replace it. This was closed in 1919 when it was deemed unsafe, and it fell into the river in 1920. A steel bridge was built in its place in 1921 and was replaced by the current bridge in 1969.

18. Piscataquog Village was centered at the intersection of what is now South Main and Varney Streets on the west side of Manchester. It was part of Bedford until 1853, when it was annexed by Manchester. The boathouse was located near the mouth of the Piscataquog River, where it intersected with the Merrimack River.

CHAPTER 7

19. Browne, *Amoskeag Manufacturing Co.*, 54.
20. Ibid., 52.

CHAPTER 8

21. Potter, *History of Manchester*, 552.
22. Steinberg, *Nature Incorporated*, 83.
23. Browne, *Amoskeag Manufacturing Co.*, 128.
24. Thoreau, *A Week on the Concord and Merrimack Rivers*, Wednesday.
25. Ibid., Tuesday.
26. Browne, *Amoskeag Manufacturing Co.*, 58.

CHAPTER 9

27. The Amory Manufacturing Company was founded in 1879. The company was named after William Amory (1804–1883) of Boston, who had served as president of the Amoskeag Manufacturing Company and as an officer of several of the other corporations in the mill yard. The massive Amory Mill along the Upper Canal was completed in 1880. The building, which is now 150 Dow Street, has two towers and is 520 feet long. The Amory Manufacturing Company was acquired by the Amoskeag Manufacturing Company in 1905.
28. The Langdon Mills corporation was founded in 1860. The company built two mills at the north end of the mill yard, where it specialized in producing cotton sheetings and shirtings. The Amory Manufacturing Company eventually took over the Langdon Mills. One of its mill buildings remains, Langdon Mill No. 2 (1868), which today is 155 Dow Street.
29. Urban renewal is the rehabilitation and rebuilding of urban areas that typically involves demolition of old structures that are no longer considered useful.
30. Langenbach, "Amoskeag Millyard."
31. Ezekiel Albert Straw (1819–1892) was agent of the Amoskeag Manufacturing Company from 1856 to 1885. His son Herman Foster

Straw (1849–1929) also was the agent of the Amoskeag from 1885 to 1919. Herman's son William Parker Straw (1878–1953) served in the same position from 1919 to 1929. After 1929, William was an officer of the Amoskeag Bank in Manchester (which was not affiliated with the Amoskeag Manufacturing Company). William became the agent of Amoskeag Industries in 1936 and was instrumental in the success of that corporation. (See Chapter 10, Note 35.)

32. Starting in the late nineteenth century, the north end of Elm Street and the side streets in that area developed into a fashionable neighborhood where the wealthier families of Manchester built impressive homes.

33. Hareven and Langenbach, *Amoskeag*, "Families."

Chapter 10

34. Thoreau, *A Week on the Concord and Merrimack Rivers*, Wednesday. The museum was located on the west side of Elm Street, across from Merrimack Common.

35. Ezekiel A. (Albert) Straw worked for the Amoskeag Manufacturing Company for forty years and was hugely influential in its success. He was born in Salisbury, New Hampshire, in 1819. His family moved to Lowell, Massachusetts, when he was a small boy. He graduated from Lowell High School and then studied mathematics at Phillips Academy in Andover, Massachusetts. In the spring of 1838, he was hired by the Lowell and Nashua Railroad as an assistant engineer. The Amoskeag Manufacturing Company asked him to come to Manchester to work temporarily as an engineer. He started with the company on July 4, 1838, when he was only eighteen years old. After drafting the street layout of the central part of the new center of Manchester, Straw decided to stay in Manchester. He worked as a civil engineer on the Amoskeag's water power projects and was named agent of the Amoskeag's Land and Water Power Company in 1851. (The Amoskeag corporation was organized into separate sub-entities at this time according to function, each with its own agent or other senior manager.) In 1856, he was given management responsibility for the manufacturing operations, and in 1858, he was given the same for the Machine Shop. With these additional responsibilities, he became the sole agent for the entire company. In 1859, Straw started the manufacture of Amoskeag Steam Fire Engines. After the Civil War, he led the Amoskeag's successful effort to create a gingham operation. Straw was involved in the community, serving on city committees and commissions. He was president of the Manchester Gas Light Company and the New Hampshire Fire Insurance Company and had financial interests in several Manchester business enterprises. An early member of the

Republican Party, he had the honor of meeting Abraham Lincoln when he visited Manchester in March 1860. Straw was elected as a state representative four times and twice as state senator, serving as Senate president in his second term. He was elected governor of New Hampshire in 1872 and again in 1873. Straw built an impressive brick mansion in Manchester that still exists at 25 Brook Street. He was forced to retire from public life due to ill health in 1879, and he died in 1882 at the age of sixty-two. Ezekiel Straw is buried in the family plot in the Valley Cemetery in Manchester.

36. Clarke, *Manchester*, 29.

CHAPTER 11

37. Browne, *Amoskeag Manufacturing Co.*, 70.
38. Ibid., 62.

CHAPTER 12

39. The Old Mill and the Bell Mill would be destroyed by fire in 1847.
40. Ibid., 72.
41. Denim is a durable cotton cloth that has a twill weaving that produces its characteristic diagonal ribbing. In May 1873, Jacob Davis and Levi Strauss patented a design for sturdy denim work pants that used metal rivets to prevent tears in places where the fabric was subject to strain. This was a major improvement over the standard denim pants, called "waist overalls," that had existed for many years. Levi Strauss & Co. began manufacturing what would become known as the "blue jean" in San Francisco later in 1873, with denim made by the Amoskeag Manufacturing Company. It is not known which of the Amoskeag's mills produced this denim.
42. The Corliss steam engine, in its many variations, was based on a design patented in 1849 by George Henry Corliss in Providence, Rhode Island.
43. The McGregor Bridge was destroyed in the flood of 1936 and replaced in 1937 with the Notre Dame Bridge, known for its graceful arches. This bridge was replaced in 1989 by the current Bridge Street Bridge.
44. The Jefferson Mill, built in 1886, was the first mill building that was constructed with its own steam power plant. The building, which is known for its distinctive clock tower, is now 670 North Commercial Street.
45. T. (Thomas) Jefferson Coolidge (1831–1920) of Boston was the great-grandson of U.S. president Thomas Jefferson. He served as treasurer of the Amoskeag Manufacturing Company from 1876 to 1880 and 1884 to 1892 and as president of the board of directors from 1901 to 1911.

Chapter 14

46. Browne, *Amoskeag Manufacturing Co.*, 77.
47. Potter, *History of Manchester*, 563.

Chapter 16

48. See Chapter 10, Note 35.
49. Browne, *Amoskeag Manufacturing Co.*, 79.
50. Ibid.

Chapter 18

51. The Cooper Union (the Cooper Union for the Advancement of Science and Art) was founded in 1859 in New York City by industrialist and inventor Peter Cooper as a free college that was open to all.
52. Page, *Abraham Lincoln in New Hampshire*, 46.
53. Poore and Eaton, *Sketches…Frederick Smyth*, 99.
54. Browne, *Amoskeag Manufacturing Co.*, 157–58.
55. Poore and Eaton, *Sketches...Frederick Smyth*, 100.
56. Ibid., 101.

Chapter 19

57. Joseph Kidder papers, Manchester Historic Association.
58. Ibid.
59. Browne, *Amoskeag Manufacturing Co.*, 82.
60. Undated news clipping in the archives of the Manchester Historic Association.
61. *Manchester Daily American*, May 22, 1863.
62. Browne, *Amoskeag Manufacturing Co.*, 82.

Chapter 20

63. Thorp, *Manchester of Yesterday*, 436.
64. Ibid., 441.
65. Hareven and Langenbach, *Amoskeag*, "First Generation."

Chapter 21

66. See Chapter 12, Note 42.
67. *New Hampshire Sunday News*, "'Big Jumbo' Mill Crash Happened 57 Years Ago," October 10, 1948.

Chapter 22

68. *Manchester Union Leader*, "Flood of '36: 'Terrible,' 'The End of the World,'" March 18, 1986.

Chapter 23

69. Mary Ann Partridge letter, Manchester Historic Association.
70. Browne, *Amoskeag Manufacturing Co.*, 135.
71. Hareven and Langenbach, *Amoskeag*, "The Setting."
72. Browne, *Amoskeag Manufacturing Co.*, 168.

Chapter 24

73. Hareven, *Family Time and Industrial Time*, 226.
74. Hareven and Langenbach, *Amoskeag*, "The World of Work."
75. Amoskeag employment records, 1911–36, Manchester Historic Association.

Chapter 25

76. Hareven and Langenbach, *Amoskeag*, "The World of Work."
77. "City of Manchester, N.H. and the Amoskeag Manufacturing Co.," 1912.

Chapter 26

78. Frederic C. Dumaine was born in 1866 in Hadley, Massachusetts. His association with the Amoskeag Manufacturing Company began in 1880, when he was hired as an office boy for T. Jefferson Coolidge (see Chapter 12, Note 45). In 1898, Dumaine was appointed treasurer of the Amory Manufacturing Company, and in 1905, he became treasurer for the Amoskeag Manufacturing Company. The treasurer essentially served as the chief executive officer of the company (while the agent functioned in a similar way to a chief operating officer). After the Amoskeag split into two trusts in 1925, Dumaine held the treasurer position in both entities. He died in 1951 in Groton, Massachusetts.
79. *Amoskeag Bulletin* (Manchester, NH), July 1, 1914.

Chapter 27

80. Hanlan, "Working Population of Manchester," 170–71.
81. *Springfield Leader*, March 12, 1922.
82. "History of Amoskeag Strike," 1. "Piece rate" is the rate of pay based on the amount of product produced.
83. Ibid., 170.
84. Hareven, *Family Time and Industrial Time*, 312.
85. "History of Amoskeag Strike," 81–82.
86. Ibid., 82.
87. Ibid., 83.
88. Ibid., 88.

Chapter 28

89. *Manchester Leader and Evening Union*, "Amoskeag Moves to Reorganize," December 24, 1935, late edition.
90. Mongan, "Community Long Pained by Loss of Its Top Employer." John C. Mongan was mayor of Manchester in 1962–63 and 1968–69.

Chapter 29

91. "The Truth about Manchester," 1936.
92. The remnants of Northern Division Power House and a 1937 addition now form the office building at 780 North Commercial Street.
93. *Boston Traveler*, "Death of Amoskeag Blessing," January 9, 1937.
94. *Evening Times*, "Business Men to See Results of Work in Athens," December 2, 1937.
95. *Manchester Union, 75th Anniversary Edition*, "A Year and a Half," March 29, 1938.

Chapter 30

96. The records of the stockholders and officers of the company are held at the Baker Library at the Harvard Business School in Cambridge, Massachusetts.

BIBLIOGRAPHY

Blood, Grace Holbrook. *Manchester on the Merrimack: The Story of a City*. Manchester, NH: Lew A. Cummings Co., 1948. Repr., Manchester Historic Association, 1975.

Browne, George Waldo. *The Amoskeag Manufacturing Co. of Manchester, New Hampshire: A History*. Manchester, NH: Amoskeag Manufacturing Company, 1915.

"City of Manchester, N.H. and the Amoskeag Manufacturing Co." (French title: "Ville de Manchester, N.H. et L'Amoskeag Manufacturing Company.") Booklet published by Amoskeag Manufacturing Company in conjunction with Manchester Chamber of Commerce, Manchester, NH, 1912.

Clarke, John B., ed. *Manchester: A Brief Record of Its Past and a Picture of Its Present*. Manchester, NH: John B. Clarke, 1875.

Creamer, Daniel B., and Charles W. Coulter. *Labor and the Shut-down of the Amoskeag Textile Mills*. Philadelphia: Works Progress Administration, National Research Project, 1939. Repr., New York: Arno & New York Times, 1971.

Gerber, Bill. "Locks and Canals of the Merrimack River." Middlesex Canal Association (Billerica, MA). *Towpath Topics* 47, no. 2. (January 2009).

Hanlan, James P. "The Working Population of Manchester, 1840–1886." Dissertation manuscript, Clark University, Worcester, MA, 1979.

Hareven, Tamara K. *Family Time and Industrial Time: The Relationship between the Family and Work in a New England Industrial Community*. Cambridge, UK: Cambridge University Press, 1993.

Hareven, Tamara K., and Randolph Langenbach. *Amoskeag: Life and Work in an American Factory-City*. New York: Pantheon Books, Random House, 1978. Repr., Lebanon, NH: University Press of New England, 1995.

———. "Remembering Life in a Mill Town." *Boston Sunday Globe*, September 17, 1978.

History of Amoskeag Strike during the Year 1922. Manchester, NH: Amoskeag Manufacturing Company, 1924.

Howard, Cynthia, AIA. *The Amoskeag: Standards for Rehabilitation within the Amoskeag Corporation Housing Historic District—Manchester, New Hampshire.* Manchester, NH: Amoskeag Neighborhood Association, 1981.

Kenison, Arthur. *Dumaine's Amoskeag: Let the Record Speak*. Manchester, NH: Saint Anselm College Press, 1997.

———. *Frederic C. Dumaine: Office Boy to Tycoon*. Manchester, NH: Saint Anselm College Press, 2000.

Langenbach, Randolph. "The Amoskeag Millyard: An Epic in Urban Design." *Harvard Alumni Bulletin* 70, no. 12 (April 13, 1968).

Mausolf, Lisa. "Survey of the Amoskeag Millyard Potential Historic District." Unpublished manuscript submitted to the New Hampshire Division of Historical Resources, 2000.

Mongan, John C. "Community Long Pained by Loss of Its Top Employer," *New Hampshire Sunday News*, February 21, 1993.

Page, Elwin L. *Abraham Lincoln in New Hampshire.* Boston: Houghton Mifflin Company, 1929.

Poore, Perley, and F.B. Eaton, eds. *Sketches of the Life and Public Service of Frederick Smyth of New Hampshire.* Manchester, NH: John B. Clarke, 1885.

Potter, C. (Chandler) E. *The History of Manchester, Formerly Derryfield, in New-Hampshire; Including That of Ancient Amoskeag, or the Middle Merrimack Valley; Together with the Address, Poem, and Other Proceedings, of the Centennial Celebration, of the Incorporation of Derryfield; at Manchester, October 22, 1851*. Manchester, NH: C.E. Potter, Publisher, 1856.

Rivard, Paul E. *A New Order of Things: How the Textile Industry Transformed New England.* Lebanon, NH: University Press of New England, 2002.

Steinberg, Theodore. *Nature Incorporated: Industrialization and the Waters of New England*. Cambridge, UK: Cambridge University Press, 1991.

Thoreau, Henry David. *A Week on the Concord and Merrimack Rivers*. New York: Library of America, 1985. Originally published 1849.

Thorp, L. (Louis) Ashton. *Manchester of Yesterday.* Manchester, NH: Granite State Press, 1939.

"The Truth about Manchester." Booklet published by Manchester Citizen's Committee on Amoskeag Affairs, August 10, 1936.

INDEX

A

Abbott, Mayor Theodore T. 134
Abenaki 16
ACA tickings. *See* textiles
Accident Department 120
Albany, New York 81
Algonquian language 16
Allegheny, Pennsylvania 92
Almy & Brown 20
American Emigrant Company 99
American Federation of Labor 138
American Locomotive Company 82
American Revolution (Revolutionary War) 18, 63, 155
Amory Manufacturing Company 46, 127, 157, 161
Amory, William 66, 99, 157
Amoskeag Axe Company 83
Amoskeag Bank 158
Amoskeag Bulletin 120, 131
Amoskeag Canal 36, 63
Amoskeag Company 143
Amoskeag Corporation Housing Historic District 154
Amoskeag Cotton and Woolen Manufacturing Company 21, 22, 23
Amoskeag Cotton and Wool Manufactory, Proprietors of the 21
Amoskeag Falls 8, 9, 15, 16, 17, 18, 20, 23, 24, 25, 27, 28, 31, 32, 33, 34, 35, 36, 40, 42, 55, 105, 129, 153, 155, 156
Amoskeag Falls Lock and Canal Company 32
Amoskeag gingham. *See* textiles
Amoskeag hose carriage 78
Amoskeag Industries, Inc. 148, 149, 150
Amoskeag Inn 27
Amoskeag Land and Water Power Company 158
Amoskeag Machine Shop 10, 45, 53, 73, 74, 75, 77, 80, 90, 91, 92, 93, 158
Amoskeag Manufacturing Company
  bankruptcy 108, 143–146
  original company founded 23
  reorganization
    1911 128
    1925 143
Amoskeag Millyard 8, 14, 151, 152, 153, 154, 155

Amoskeag Pond 34, 35
Amoskeag Reservoir 84
Amoskeag rifle muskets 93–94
Amoskeag Steam Fire Engine 10, 77, 80, 81, 82, 158
  Amoskeag No. 1 80
  Ashland No. 1 82
  Engine Six (Cambridge, Massachusetts) 81
  General Grant 92
  Lafayette 1 81
  Princess Alexandra 81
  Queen Victoria 81
Amoskeag steam locomotive engines 75–76
  Etna 75
  General Stark 75
  rail lines served 75, 76
  Washington 75
Amoskeag—Success Story film 149
Amoskeag Textile Club 117, 118, 120, 122, 131
Amoskeag Textile School 120
Amoskeag Village 22, 25, 26, 27, 28, 30, 31, 32, 34, 55, 61, 65, 68, 156
Anchor Manufacturing Company 150
Andover, Massachusetts 58
Arms Park 73
Arms Textile Manufacturing Company 150
Ashland, Massachusetts 82
Athens, Pennsylvania 149
Atlantic Ocean 9, 15, 16
Australia 81

B

bags, seamless 64, 92, 129
Baker Library, Harvard Business School 162
Baldwin, Cyrus 64
Bass, Governor Robert P. 124
Bean, Nehemiah S. 77, 78, 80, 81, 82, 93
Bedford, New Hampshire 21, 61, 157
Big Jumbo Steam Engine 102
Black, Arthur 146, 148
Black Brook 18
Blackstone River 9
Bliss, Fabyan & Co. 131
Blodget (Blodgett), Samuel 7, 18, 21, 30, 34, 156
Blodget's canal 27, 31, 33, 34, 35, 36, 37, 39
Boston Associates 29, 32, 33, 35
Boston, Massachusetts 18, 23, 26, 27, 29, 53, 57, 75, 80, 81, 145, 148, 157, 159
Boston Red Sox 121, 122
Boucher, Marie-Anna (St. Denis) 111
Bow Canal 33
Bow, New Hampshire 25, 33
Brannan, Daniel 25
Brewer, Gardner 99
bridges
  Amoskeag Bridge (at Amoskeag Falls) 108
  Bass Island Bridge 108
  Bridge Street Bridge 39, 152, 159
  covered bridge 26, 41, 48
  footbridge 41, 108
  Granite Street Bridge 31, 105, 107, 108
  McGregor Bridge 68, 108, 135, 159
  McGregor Bridge (original 1792) 68
  Notre Dame Bridge 159
  Queen City Bridge 108
Browne, George Waldo 7, 8, 23, 26, 30, 37, 63, 73, 80, 81, 90
Brown, Governor Albert O. 138
Brugger, John 84, 88
Bunker, Samuel J. 102

C

Cambridge, Massachusetts 81
Canada 11, 76, 81, 82, 113, 123, 141
Canis, Augustus 99
Canterbury, New Hampshire 77
Caron, Mayor Damase 108
Carpenter, Frank P. 147, 148
Carson, F. Frank 16

Central Division 39, 41, 48, 72
Central Division Power Plant 41
Central Fire Station 79, 107
Chelmsford, Massachusetts 49, 73
Chester, New Hampshire 25
Chicago, Illinois 88, 131, 132
Chicopee Manufacturing Company 150
Chicopee, Massachusetts 29
child labor 123–126
Chile 81
China 81
Citizens Preparedness Parade, 1916 132
City Hotel 87
Civil War 10, 71, 90, 91, 93, 95, 113, 158
Clarke, John B. 61
Cocheco Land & Water Company 35
Collins, Sally 25
Concord Common 58, 79
Concord Manufacturing Company 33
Concord, Massachusetts 35
Concord, New Hampshire 15, 18, 26, 75, 86, 87
Concord River 35
Concord Square 58
Coolidge, Thomas Jefferson 68, 159, 161
Cooper, Peter 160
Cooper Union (Cooper Union for the Advancement of Science and Art) 86, 87, 160
Coos Brook 18
Corliss engine 67, 102, 159
Corliss, George Henry 159
corporate paternalism 118, 120
Cram, Ada L. 102
Cunion, Mary 100
Cunion, Susan 100

D

dams
  1840 34
  1871 (arch dam) 40, 41, 42, 105
  Amoskeag Dam (1921) 42, 45, 106, 107
Davie, John S.B. 138
Davis, Harry L. 148
Davis, Jacob 159
Dean, Caroline 23
Dean, Dr. Oliver 23, 24, 25, 28
Democrats 87
Derryfield, New Hampshire 17, 18, 21, 31, 155, 156
Derry, New Hampshire 17
Detroit, Michigan 81
Dignam, Walter 91, 92
Dorrs Pond 62
Douglas, Stephen 86
Dover, New Hampshire 29, 88
Dumaine, F. (Frederic) C. 131, 132, 138, 144, 145, 161
Dunbarton, New Hampshire 25
Dunstable (now Nashua), New Hampshire 23

E

Edmond, Catherine 99
eels 17, 18
employment office 119, 120, 125, 128, 130, 135
England 11, 18, 20, 95, 99
Essex Manufacturing Company 77
Europe 19, 57, 95, 123, 130, 133, 137
Exeter, New Hampshire 86, 88

F

Fabyan, George 131, 132
Fall River, Massachusetts 141
family names
  Amory 29
  Appleton 29
  Archibald 25
  Barrett 31
  Cabot 29
  Clark 31
  Davis 31
  Gamble 31
  Hall 31
  Jackson 29, 31

Kidder 31
Lawrence 29
Lowell 29
Merrill 31
Rowell 31
Stark 31
Stevens 31
Wilson 31
firemen's muster (1859) 80
First New Hampshire Battery 94
First New Hampshire Volunteer Regiment 92
Fishing Islands 15, 24
Fitchburg, Massachusetts 144
Flanders, Mary (Straw) 54
flax 19
floods 105–108
Flywheel Disaster, 1891 102–104
Fort Sumter, South Carolina 90
foundry 49, 68, 73, 74
Fourth New Hampshire Volunteer Regiment 91
Foye, Frank A. 139
Foye, Police Sergeant William 139
Franconia Notch, New Hampshire 15
Franklin, New Hampshire 15, 35
Franklin Street School 54
French and Indian War 155

G

Garvin's Falls 33
gatehouse 34, 37, 40, 41, 45, 106, 107
Gay, Ira 23, 28
Germany 11, 99
Gill Stadium 62, 122
Gilmanton, New Hampshire 77
Glasgow, Scotland 99, 100
Goffe's Falls 108
Goffstown, New Hampshire 20, 25, 55, 61, 156
Gompers, Samuel 138
Granite Fusiliers 61
Great Boston Fire, 1872 81
Great Britain 18, 19, 22, 92, 116
Great Depression 9, 141, 149
Great Exhibition in London, 1851 95
Great Sawmill—the Industry 18
Greece 11
Groton, Massachusetts 161
Guertin, Bishop George Albert 138

H

Hadley, Massachusetts 161
Hampton Beach, New Hampshire 120
Hanlan, James P. 134
Hareven, Tamara K. 7, 100, 120, 125, 138
Harvey, Jonas 20
Haverhill, Massachusetts 16, 156
Hayes, Mrs. Anna 60
Healy, Chief of Police M.J. 139, 140
Heritage Commission, City of Manchester 154
herring 17
Hine, Lewis Wickes 47, 124
Holyoke, Massachusetts 29
Honolulu, Hawaii 92
Hood, Robert 99
Hooksett Falls 33
Hooksett Manufacturing Company 33
Hooksett, New Hampshire 25, 33, 36, 46, 55, 69
Hooksett Village 107
hosiery manufacturing 84, 88, 92
hydroelectric plant 43, 45, 106, 107, 147, 149

I

Illinois 86
immigrants (see also by name of country)
English 17, 99, 109, 116
Franco-American 8, 113, 125
French-Canadian 113, 122
German 84, 99, 116
Greek 116
Irish 112, 116
Lithuanian 116
Polish 116

Russian 116
Scots-Irish 17, 19
Scottish 99, 100, 109, 116
Swedish 112, 116
Industrial Revolution 18
International Cotton Mills 138
Ireland 11
Isle of Hooksett Canal 33

J

Jefferson, President Thomas 159
Jewel, Edmund 147
J.F. McElwain Company 150
Johnson & Johnson 150

K

Kane, Mary 102
Kidder, Joseph 90, 92
Kidder, Samuel P. 21
Knights of Labor 136

L

Laconia, New Hampshire 15
Lafayette Park 122
Lake Winnipesaukee 15, 35
lamprey 17
Lancashire, England 99
Langdon Mills 46, 110, 157
Langenbach, Randolph 7, 39, 50, 100, 120
Latham, George 86, 88
Lawrence, Massachusetts 16, 29, 35, 75, 77, 78
Lawrence No. 7 80
Levi Strauss & Co. 159
Lincoln, Abraham 65, 86, 87, 88, 89, 159
Lincoln, Robert Todd 86, 88
Lindner, Edward (Eduard) 94
Lithuania 11
Little Canada 122
Londonderry, New Hampshire 17, 19
London, England 81, 95
Lowell and Nashua Railroad 58
Lowell High School 158
Lowell, Massachusetts 15, 16, 18, 28, 29, 35, 36, 77, 112, 158
Lower Canal 36, 37, 39, 40, 42, 66, 73, 83, 102, 151

M

Maine 76, 81
Manchester Chamber of Commerce 16, 128
Manchester Citizens' Committee on Amoskeag Affairs 147
Manchester City Hall 58, 61
Manchester Electric Light Company 85
Manchester, England 18
Manchester Gas Light Company 158
Manchester Historic Association 8, 102, 153
Manchester House 59, 60
Manchester Knitted Fashions, Inc. 150
Manchester Locomotive Works 76, 82
Manchester Mills 46, 69, 71, 72, 127, 155
Manchester, New Hampshire
development of city 55–62
name change from Derryfield 21
Manchester Print Works 46, 69, 70, 71, 87, 88, 92, 109, 134, 136
Manchester's town hall (city hall) 61
Manchester Traction, Light and Power Company 85
Manning Boiler 42, 43
Manning, Charles H. 42, 103, 104
Manufacturers' League 121, 122
March of Time film 149
Marshall Field & Company 132
Marshall, Harlan A. 131
Massachusetts 17, 20, 23, 35, 141
McDonald, Reverend William 112
McGregor Farm 23
McGregor, Reverend David 17, 156
McGregor, Robert 68, 156
McGregorville 61, 68
McIntire, David J. 139
McKay sewing machines 92
McLane, Attorney John 147, 148
McQuesten, David 21

Mechanics' Mills 83
Mechanics' Row 83, 84, 85
Medway, Massachusetts 23
Merrimack Common 58, 59, 60, 80, 158
Merrimack Mills 46, 69
Merrimack, New Hampshire 36
Merrimack River 8, 9, 10, 15, 18, 20, 27, 28, 30, 31, 32, 33, 35, 36, 37, 40, 41, 46, 48, 55, 56, 60, 65, 68, 72, 73, 74, 84, 96, 103, 105, 107, 135, 145, 150, 153, 155, 157
Merrimack Square 58
Middlesex Canal 18
Mill Girl statue 152
mills (Manchester—see also company names)
- Amory Mill 40, 125, 157
- Bag Mill 67
- Bell Mill 22, 23, 24, 28, 65, 159
- Coolidge Mill 42, 54, 67, 68, 122, 125, 139, 140, 150
- Island Mill 24, 65
- Jefferson Mill 67, 68, 85, 105, 106, 114, 153, 159
- Langdon Mill No. 2 157
- Mill No. 2 (Manchester Print Works, Manchester Mills) 69, 71, 72
- Mill No. 4 102
- Mill No. 10 (Southern Division) 72
- Mill No. 11 68, 110, 122, 125, 131
- Mill Nos. 4 and 5 39, 48, 67
- New Bag Mill 68
- New Print Works 72
- No. 1 Amoskeag New Mill 65, 66, 67
- No. 2 Amoskeag New Mill 65, 66, 67
- No. 3 Amoskeag New Mill (Mill No. 3) 66, 67, 154
- Old Mill 23, 65, 159
- Pandora Mill 71
- Stark Mill 47, 64, 65, 152
- Stark Mill No. 1 63
- Waumbec Mill 67

Millyard Museum 82, 91, 154
Milwaukee, Wisconsin 92
Mohawks 36
Molloy, Bert 125
Mongan, former mayor John C. 146
Moreau, former mayor Arthur 147, 148
Mount Washington 35
Mungall, Andrew 96, 100
Mungall, Robert 100
Mungall, Samuel 100
Mungall, Thomas 100

N

Nashua, New Hampshire 15, 16, 23, 29
National Child Labor Committee (NCLC) 123, 124
National Geographic 133
National Register of Historic Places 61
Native American 129
New Bedford, Massachusetts 141
Newburyport, Massachusetts 15
New England 19, 25, 42, 71, 75, 80, 92, 94, 105, 113, 123, 129, 130, 137, 138, 141, 142
New England Weston Electric Light Company 84, 85
New Hampshire 15, 18, 20, 21, 25, 35, 46, 107, 120, 124, 128, 129, 136, 138, 141, 147, 149, 159
New Hampshire Fire Insurance Company 158
New Hampshire legislature 21, 28, 37, 124, 138
New Hampshire National Guard 107, 141
New Hampshire State Armory 141
New Ipswich, New Hampshire 20
New Orleans, Louisiana 81
New York, New York 81, 86, 92, 94, 123, 132, 160
No. 2 Mill (Manchester Print Works, Manchester Mills) 70
Normandin, Fred 124
north end (of Manchester) 54
Northern Division 72

Northern Division Power House 42, 72, 149, 162
Northern Ireland 17
Notre Dame neighborhood 114
Nutfield 17, 156

O

Olzendam, Abraham P. 84
Oregon 81

P

Page, Elwin L. 87
Palace Theatre 138
Pan-American Conference 102
Pandora Industries 150
Parker, James 21
Parkhill Manufacturing Company 144
Park Theatre 138
Partridge, Mary Ann 109
Pawtucket, Rhode Island 9, 20
Pellerin, Jules 126
Pellerin, Valeda (Cora) (Tourigny) 125, 126
Pemigewasset River 15, 35
Penacook Indians 16
Pennsylvania 136
Peru 81
Peterborough, New Hampshire 124
Peterson, Bishop John B. 145
Phenix Hall 86
Philadelphia, Pennsylvania 80, 81
Phillips Academy 158
Phillips Exeter Academy 86
Pike, Francis Harvey "Saxie" 91, 92
Piscataquog River 18, 157
Piscataquog Village 27, 61, 156, 157
Pitcher, Larned 23, 28
Pittsburgh, Pennsylvania 81
Poland 11
Portland, Maine 76
Potter, C. (Chandler) E. 32, 74
Preparedness Movement 132
Prichard, Benjamin 20, 21
Profile Lake 15
Protestant clergy 138
Providence, Rhode Island 22
Public Service Company of New Hampshire 45, 85, 147, 149
Puritans 17

Q

Quebec 113, 125, 129

R

Rand, Willard D. 148
Red Gate House 37
Reid, James 99
Reps Dry Goods Co. 137
Republicans 86, 87, 88, 124, 159
Rhode Island 20, 23, 141
Richard, Eliphalet 25
Richardson, Edwin P. 88
Riviere, Horace A. 140
Robinson, Olney 22, 23
Rock Rimmon 122
Rock Rimmon Park 122
Rogers Rangers 155
Rogier, William 107
Roman Catholics 59, 112, 113, 138, 145
Roosevelt, President Theodore 133
Russia 11, 81, 94, 116

S

Sachem Wannalancet 35
Saco, Maine 29
S.A. Felton & Company 83
Salisbury, Massachusetts 23
Salisbury, New Hampshire 158
salmon 17, 23
San Francisco, California 81, 159
Saxony, Germany 99
Sayles, Willard 23, 28
Sayre, Pennsylvania 149
Schiller, Avery 147
Scotland 11, 17, 95, 99, 100, 127
Scott, Thomas 78, 80
Seekonk, Massachusetts 23
Seventh Regiment band 132

shad 17
Shakers 77
Shaw, Edward 61
Shepherd's Tavern 59, 60, 66
Shepherd, William 59
Silver Brothers Company, Inc. 150
Sisters of Mercy 112
Slater Mill 9
Slater, Samuel 19, 20, 22, 23, 28
Smithfield, Rhode Island 22
Smith, Thomas "Tommy" 127
Smyth, Frederick 86, 87, 88, 89
Smyth Hall 87
Smyth's Block 87
South Carolina 90
Southern Division 10, 72
South Main Street firehouse 107
Special Model 1861 rifle muskets 93
Spinney, Frank O. 102
Springfield, Illinois 87, 137
Springfield, Massachusetts 93
St. Anne Parish 112
Stark Guards 61
Stark, John, Jr. 21, 156
Stark, Major General John 18, 31, 63, 155, 156
Stark Manufacturing Company 46, 59, 63, 64, 65, 92, 112, 127, 134, 136, 138
Starr, James 140
Ste. Marie Parish 113
Stevens, Captain Phinehas 65
Stevens, Ephraim 20
Stevens, Robert 20
St. Louis, Missouri 132
Stokes, Benjamin S. 83
Strauss, Levi 159
Straw, Ezekiel Albert 58, 77, 81, 82, 88, 92, 93, 94, 95, 98, 99, 100, 157, 158, 159
Straw, Herman Foster 158
Straw School 54
Straw, William Parker 53, 54, 137, 146, 148, 158
streets (Manchester)
  25 Brook Street 159
  33 South Commercial Street 72
  55 South Commercial Street 72
  88 Commercial Street 71
  150 Dow Street 40, 157
  155 Dow Street 157
  186 Granite Street 72
  195 McGregor Street 68, 131
  200 Bedford Street 67, 154
  250 Commercial Street 48, 67
  286 Commercial Street 100
  300 Bedford Street 65
  324 Commercial Street 100
  340 Commercial Street 100
  345 McGregor Street 68
  387 Canal Street 135
  400 Bedford Street 64
  400 Commercial Street 73
  540 North Commercial Street 68
  670 North Commercial Street 67, 159
  780 North Commercial Street 162
  Amherst Street 79
  Amory Street 139
  Bedford Street 39, 69, 87
  Blodget Street 84
  Canal Street 40, 51, 52, 53, 64, 76, 79, 119, 120, 121, 127, 141, 151
  Chestnut Street 60
  Commercial Street 39, 40, 69, 151
  Concord Street 60
  Coolidge Avenue 122
  Elm Street 53, 58, 59, 60, 61, 66, 87, 158
  Franklin Street 53
  Granite Street 10, 56, 69, 72
  Hanover Street 59
  Harrison Street 84
  Hollis Street 52, 53
  Kidder Street 52
  Lowell Street 59, 87
  Mammoth Road 55, 60
  Market Street 61, 119
  McGregor Street 54, 139
  Mechanic Street 47

Merrimack Street 59, 60
Mungall Street 100
Oak Street 84
Pleasant Street 39, 51, 53, 54, 69, 87
River Road 54
Russell Street 84
Second Street 108
South Main Street 157
Spruce Street 54
Stark Street 39, 51, 64, 94, 119, 127, 141
Union Street 59
Valley Street 122
Varney Street 157
Vine Street 79
West Bridge Street 139, 140
strike of 1922 134–142
Sweden 11
Sweeney, Federal Judge George C. 146

T

Taunton, Massachusetts 75
Templeton, Massachusetts 109
Ten-Hour Movement 136
Textile Field 62, 121, 122
textiles
ACA tickings 24, 25, 92
Amoskeag gingham 95, 97, 98, 128, 137
calicos 70, 71, 109
cassimeres 71
cotton 9, 10, 19, 20, 21, 24, 25, 32, 63, 64, 66, 67, 68, 69, 70, 71, 74, 83, 92, 93, 95, 113, 127, 128, 129, 137, 143, 150, 154, 157, 159
denim 67, 92, 95, 159
drillings 64
drills 92
duck 64
flannels 67, 92, 95
gauze 150
ginghams 10, 19, 66, 67, 95, 96, 99, 100, 101, 116, 128, 136, 137, 144, 158
linen 19, 92
mousseline de laine (delaine) 69
muslin 69
prints 19, 92
rayon 137, 144, 148, 150
sheetings 25, 92, 95, 157
shirtings 25, 92, 157
ticking (tickings) 24, 66, 92, 95
wool (worsted) 19, 20, 25, 69, 71, 74, 83, 92, 129, 148
Textron, Incorporated 150
Thoreau, Henry David 35, 36, 55
Thoreau, John 35
Thorp, L. Ashton 100
Tiffany, Lyman 23, 28
Tourigny. *See* Pellerin

U

Ulster Scots 17
Union army 10, 91, 93
Union Locks and Canal Company 33
Union Station, Boston & Maine Railroad 56, 57
United States Armory 93
United States Army 90
United States Congress 95, 124
United Textile Workers (UTW) 136, 138, 139, 140, 141, 142
University of New Hampshire 153
Upper Canal 36, 37, 39, 40, 42, 63, 65, 66, 67, 151, 157

V

Valley Cemetery 62, 159
Varick Park 122
Varney School 98
Veterans Memorial Park 58
Victory Park 58

W

Waltham-Lowell system 29
Waltham, Massachusetts 29
Warde, Mother Frances Xavier 112

War of 1812 22
Washington, D.C. 92, 93, 94, 137
Waumbec Mills, Inc. 150
Weare, New Hampshire 25
White Mountains 15, 35, 105
Winnipesaukee Lake Company 35
Winnipesaukee River 15, 35
W.M. Auclair 150
Women's Aid and Relief Society 59
workers' housing 29, 46, 47, 49, 50, 53, 54, 58, 59, 87, 99, 147, 149, 153
Works Progress Administration (WPA) 107, 108
World War I 7, 130, 133, 137
World War II 150

ABOUT THE AUTHOR

Aurore (Dionne) Eaton is a native of Manchester, New Hampshire. She grew up in the Franco-American neighborhood on Manchester's west side and attended grammar school at St. Jean-Baptiste (St. John the Baptist) parish on Kelley Street. She graduated from Pembroke Academy in Pembroke, New Hampshire, and earned a bachelor of fine arts degree from Colby-Sawyer College in New London, New Hampshire. She also studied theater design at Dartmouth College in Hanover, New Hampshire. She is the former executive director of the Manchester Historic Association and of the Cambridge (Massachusetts) Historical Society. Aurore has researched and promoted Manchester's history for over twenty-five years. She writes a weekly column, "Looking Back," for the *New Hampshire Union Leader* newspaper that focuses on New Hampshire history.

Aurore Eaton in the Millyard Museum standing next to the Ashland No. 1 Amoskeag Steam Fire Engine. *Photograph by Stephen J. Garczynski.*

Visit us at
www.historypress.net

This title is also available as an e-book